BULLY SECOND EDITION
PREVENTION

BULLY PREVENTION

SECOND EDITION

Tips and Strategies for School Leaders and Classroom Teachers

ELIZABETH A. BARTON

CORWIN PRESS
A SAGE Publications Company
Thousand Oaks, California

For information:

Corwin Press, Inc.
A Sage Publications Company
2455 Teller Road
Thousand Oaks, California 91320
www.corwinpress.com

Sage Publications Ltd.
1 Oliver's Yard
55 City Road
London EC1Y 1SP
United Kingdom

Sage Publications India Pvt. Ltd.
B-42, Panchsheel Enclave
Post Box 4109
New Delhi 110 017 India

Printed in the United States of America.

This book is printed on acid-free paper.

Library of Congress Cataloging-in-Publication Data

Barton, Elizabeth A. Bully prevention : tips and strategies for school leaders and classroom teachers / Elizabeth A. Barton.— 2nd ed.
      p. cm.
Includes bibliographical references and index.
ISBN 1-4129-3917-8 (cloth) — ISBN 1-4129-3918-6 (pbk.)
   1. Bullying in schools—Prevention. 2. Bullying—Prevention.
3. School violence. 4. Aggressiveness in children. I. Title.
LB3013.3.B37 2006
371.5'8—dc22

                                                    2005037815

06   07   08   09   10   10   9   8   7   6   5   4   3   2   1

Acquisitions Editor:	Cathy Hernandez
Editorial Assistant:	Charline Wu
Project Editor:	Kate Peterson
Copy Editor:	Pam Suwinsky
Typesetter:	C&M Digitals (P) Ltd.
Indexer:	Naomi Linzer
Cover Designer:	Rose Storey

Contents

Preface

The Issue of Bullying and School Safety

Increasingly, school administrators and faculty are faced with the new responsibility of creating safer schools, in addition to their traditional mission of developing academic goals and helping children reach them. Pervasive bullying in schoolyards, classrooms, and hallways interferes with perceived school safety and directly impacts student learning outcomes.

Recent studies have indicated that children today are often afraid to attend school. DeVoe and Kaffenberger (2005) reported that bullied students were more likely than nonbullied students to skip school because they thought someone might attack or harm them. Once in school, researchers cite that victims often have difficulty concentrating on schoolwork and therefore are often at risk for poor performance and ultimately school truancy or dropout. DeVoe and Kaffenberger reported that bullied students were most likely to report receiving Ds and Fs than their nonbullied counterparts. In this same study, about 4 percent of students between 12 and 18 years old carried a weapon to school for protection.

In addition, a potential relationship exists between bullying and violence in school. Research suggests that being victimized by bullying may be an antecedent to aggressive behavior (Nansel, Overpeck, et al., 2001). In 2001, the Secret Service released its comprehensive report on youth violence in schools, exposing the possibility that violent youth involved in school shootings (for example, Littleton, Colorado, and Pearl, Mississippi) share a common thread: being victims of bullying in school (Vossekuil, Fein, Reddy, Borum, & Modzeleski, 2002).

School leaders and classroom teachers have multiple reasons for addressing bullying behaviors in school. Although the threat of violence and desire for academic success are significant reasons for anti-bullying efforts, teachers and school administrators should feel compelled to intervene in bullying episodes, as it is their duty and obligation to build inclusive classroom environments for all students.

ANTI-BULLYING PROGRAMMING WITHIN A SAFE SCHOOL CONTEXT

Anti-bullying programming, like other conflict resolution education, emphasizes developing students' social skills and their ability to collaborate during conflict situations. Researchers have found that developing children's social skills has a positive impact on academic achievement, particularly with at-risk children (Johnson & Johnson, 1995b). Hence, support for social skills programming in the school is key to further developing children's cognitive capabilities in the classroom.

Education programming targeting anti-bullying has been successful in isolation in countries such as Great Britain. However, much of the work has focused on reducing bullying behaviors and not on developing the social skills of victims or changing the behavior of witnesses. Anti-bullying programming has often been viewed as a separate social skills training program rather than a piece of building safer schools. Anti-bullying programming is an integral component for building safer schools. As such, it should always be combined and consistent with other whole school approaches such as character education, specific conflict resolution programs (for example, peer mediation), and diversity education programming. The whole school approach to programming and policy will afford the school and its students the opportunity to drive organizational change so that students feel safer in the hallways and classrooms of their schools.

Bullying is not a new phenomenon or specific to the United States. The vision of the big, strong, and popular bully overpowering the weak, scrawny, and unpopular child has long been part of mainstream American culture. As adults, we vividly recall the bully-victim relationships of our childhood classrooms and neighborhoods. Europe and Scandinavia clearly identify bullying behavior as problematic for both youth and adults and have developed prevention, intervention, and public policy to ensure that bullying does not result in tragic acts of violence. Great Britain and Norway have included bully prevention in their interpretation of dictates of the United Nations Rights of the Child, which ensures the safety and welfare of all children. They consider the prevention of bullying behaviors an important component in building safer school communities.

We in the United States should join other countries in viewing bully prevention as a necessary component of safe school planning. Many schools already participate in crisis response planning and conflict resolution education. They should now consider including social skills training programs, staff development programs, and school policies on bullying behaviors to create the safest learning environment for all students.

ORGANIZATION OF THE BOOK

This book is intended to provide school leaders and K–12 classroom teachers with practical strategies and information to develop, implement, and evaluate bully prevention and intervention programs. It provides a foundation for understanding the bully-victim relationship, outlines potential origins of these behaviors, and provides applications and mechanisms for building schoolwide and classroom anti-bullying programs.

Chapter 1, The Bully, Victim, and Witness Relationship Defined, outlines these relationships and explains how conflict and aggression play a role in bullying. Trends among bullies and victims, and the long-term effects of these relationships, are discussed to emphasize the importance of prevention and intervention in classroom and school settings.

Chapter 2, Origins of Bully-Victim-Witness Behavior, describes potential sources of bullying and victim behavior. These include family, school, classroom, and individual characteristics. Understanding the complexity and origin of bullying relationship behaviors will assist school leaders and teachers in both better assessing the needs of affected youth and determining appropriate prevention and intervention techniques.

Chapter 3, Implementing the Schoolwide Anti-Bullying Program, discusses steps to implementing anti-bullying programs schoolwide. This chapter establishes the need for reviewing and/or creating policies and procedures for anti-bullying programs. It also discusses assembling an anti-bullying committee and providing a time line for implementation. The chapter provides examples of effective policies, staff development, and parent involvement techniques.

Chapter 4, Strategies for Managing and Preventing Bullying Behavior in the Classroom, outlines different techniques for the management and prevention of classroom-based bullying. The chapter describes classroom curricula and programs implemented through the process and infusion approaches. In addition to student education initiatives, this chapter explains methods teachers can use to assess their relationships with students, the classroom environment, and classroom policies that may be affecting bullying behavior among students.

Chapter 5, Strategies for Intervention, details methods for handling observed and reported bullying behaviors. The chapter covers conferencing and interviewing strategies as well as procedures for reaching out and involving parents of bullies and victims in the intervention strategy.

Chapter 6, Evaluating Anti-Bullying Initiatives, describes methods for identifying the effectiveness of classroom and schoolwide anti-bullying efforts. This chapter outlines differences in process, outcome, and impact evaluation processes and provides examples of measures that may be useful in identifying success at the individual, classroom, and school level.

Finally, Chapter 7, Legislation Regarding Bullying Behavior, covers legal implications of bullying behaviors in schools and describes statewide legislative trends.

MODIFICATIONS TO THE SECOND EDITION

The second edition of *Bullying Prevention: Tips and Strategies for School Leaders and Classroom Teachers* contains a number of modifications that will better assist school leaders and teachers with planning, implementing, and evaluating anti-bullying efforts in their schools and classrooms. Case studies and scenarios have been added throughout the book to provide real-life examples of terms and concepts presented. Updated research on issues such as relational and cyber bullying are included, along with a discussion of bullying and the special needs population. Readers are presented with additional information for teaching assertiveness and problem solving and how to infuse these concepts into the classroom setting. Finally, program evaluation has been modified for the busy school member who intends to measure the success of their programming.

Publisher's Acknowledgments

Corwin Press gratefully acknowledges the contributions of the following reviewers:

Judy Brunner, Principal
Parkview High School, Springfield, MO

Elizabeth F. Day, Sixth Grade Teacher
Mechanicville Middle School, Mechanicville, NY

Linda L. Eisinger, Third Grade Teacher
West Elementary, Jefferson City, MO

Ruth Gharst, Assistant Administrator
Heatherstone Elementary, Olathe, KS

Sandra Harris, Associate Professor
Director, Center for Doctoral Studies in Educational Leadership
Lamar University, Beaumont, TX

Deborah Johnson, Principal
Lunt School, Falmouth, ME

Patti Kinney, Principal
Talent Middle School, Talent, OR

Roseanne Lopez, Principal
Lulu Walker Elementary School, Tucson, AZ

Teresa Tulipana, Principal
Hawthorn Elementary, Kansas City, MO

About the Author

 **Elizabeth A. Barton** is associate director of the Center for Peace and Conflict Studies and Assistant Professor (Research) at Wayne State University. As a developmental psychologist specializing in socioemotional development, she has served as a national consultant on school-based violence for more than a decade. She recently received a U.S. Department of Education grant to study the effect of violence exposure on learning in a longitudinal sample of urban youth and is currently conducting a statewide assessment in Michigan of organizational readiness for youth violence prevention programs. Elizabeth is the author of numerous publications, including *Leadership Strategies for Safe Schools.* She is a Fellow of the Urban Health Initiative, a national program of the Robert Wood Johnson Foundation. She earned her PhD and MA at Wayne State University and BS at the University of Michigan.

To my son Thomas

1

The Bully, Victim, and Witness Relationship Defined

> **Maggie**
>
> Maggie has several close friends at school but is not considered popular. The girls meet early in the morning each day, have lunch together, and meet after school before going home.
>
> There is another group of girls who has a problem with one of Maggie's friends.
>
> One day after school the large group of girls surrounded Maggie's friend. They called her names and pushed her. A security guard ran toward the group, and the girls scattered. Maggie stayed to comfort her friend and walked her home from school.
>
> A few days later when Maggie arrived at school, she saw the same girls blocking her entrance to the school. They became verbally abusive and tried to trip her.
>
> The next day the girls were there again, so Maggie couldn't pass. This time they pulled at her coat and knocked her books on the ground. In the library later that week, Maggie saw a newly created

> computer screen saver with her name and face transposed onto a farm animal in a very compromising position.
>
> The next morning, Maggie was sick and didn't go to school. Her mother didn't think she seemed sick but let her stay home. When the same thing happened the next morning, Maggie's mother knew something was wrong.

Each day, students like Maggie encounter physical, verbal, and cyber bullying at the hands of classmates. Each day, students avoid going to school and create somatic symptoms because of the fear of bullying behavior. Bullying is one form of problem behavior that concerns students, teachers and administrators, and parents because of its potential impact on the students' well-being.

In this chapter, bullying behaviors are defined, connections among bullying and aggression and conflict are discussed, and trends in bullying and victimization are highlighted.

BULLYING DEFINED

Bullying is most commonly defined as a set of aggressive behaviors toward others that are characterized by three criteria:

1. Bullying is intentional aggression that may be physical, verbal, sexual, or more indirect (relational). Bullying behaviors also may be demonstrated through technology such as cell phones and computers.

2. Bullying exposes victims to repeated aggression over an extended period of time. Currently, researchers are not certain how to quantify "period of time." Specifically, it is not certain how much time it might take for bullying to impact a victim's psychological well-being.

3. Bullying occurs within an interpersonal relationship characterized by a real or perceived imbalance of power. Such power may originate from physical size or strength, or from psychological power, with children who have great peer influence exhibiting greater power in bully-victim relationships.

Research has identified bullying as ongoing, unsolicited, and frequently not physically injurious (Hoover, Oliver, & Thomson, 1993). Rather, physical and verbal bullying are only part of the school experience, and there are various sources of subtle bullying that inflicts psychological and emotional harm on victims (Batsche, 1997). In contrast to physical bullying, relational bullying involves interpersonally manipulative behaviors (Crick & Grotpeter, 1995) including direct control ("You can't be my friend unless . . ."), rejection (spreading rumors or lies), and social exclusion (excluding a peer from play or a peer relationship). Relational bullying has been found in children as young as 3 years (Crick, Casas, & Ku, 1999), while more covert forms of relational bullying have been found in middle childhood and adolescence (Yoon, Barton, & Taiariol, 2004).

Although most bully-victim relationships involve only one type of bullying, some bullies incorporate physical, verbal, sexual, and/or relational behaviors within their relationships. In our portrait of Maggie, the bully and her peer group members demonstrated physical, verbal, and a newly described form of bullying: cyber bullying.

Physical, verbal, relational, and sexual bullying behaviors may occur over an extended period of time in a variety of contexts, including the classroom, hallways, playground, or traveling to and from school. Cyber bullying allows students to continue bullying beyond the school day, through the use of cell phones and computer chat rooms.

Cyber bullies (also known as "griefers") are now using the anonymity of the Web to carry out verbal and relational bullying without seeing its effects on victims or running the risk of being discovered. The issue of cyber bullying is becoming more prevalent with the widespread use of wireless devices such as cell phones and hand-held computers. Cyber bullying is occurring more frequently in affluent suburbs across the country, where computer use is high and children are technologically adept. Long-term effects of cyber bullying have not yet been identified.

In a suburb of Chicago, several students were suspended following an incident of cyber bullying. The school discovered a sophisticated Web site on which students chose the "victim of the month." Students in the high school were provided opportunities to vote for their "favorite," who then became the target for several male bullies. In another incident, a California student accused a fellow student of using a camera phone to take inappropriate pictures of her in the locker room and then posting the pictures on a commonly viewed Web site. These are only two examples of a growing trend of cyber bullying by today's youth.

Figure 1.1 summarizes and defines types of bullying behaviors.

THE ROLE OF CONFLICT AND AGGRESSION

Bullying behaviors differ from common conflict and aggressive behaviors, and understanding the differences among conflict, aggression, and bullying is an important first step to preventing and intervening in bullying relationships in the school community.

Figure 1.1   Bullying Behaviors

Bullying behavior is intentional aggression that may be physical, verbal, relational, sexual, or demonstrated through "cyber" methods.

Physical

Hitting, kicking, punching, pushing, choking

Every day for two weeks in the beginning of the school year, Ryan would come home with bruises on his arms and neck. He told me that he played football at lunch and that it always got a little rough. I thought he must have stopped playing because the bruising stopped, but one day I saw him changing out of his school uniform and he had terrible bruises on his legs and cuts around his ankles. He finally told me that kids at school were constantly kicking and hitting him in the locker room. Just the other day they decided to practice "hog tying" his feet with strapping tape.

—Jannice, mother of Ryan (age 9)

Verbal

Threatening, teasing, name calling

My daughter Mary Jane has to wear thick glasses as a result of recent eye surgery. She was never really popular, but now she is taunted and teased every day about the way she looks. Several students just won't leave her alone.

—Meredith, mother of Mary Jane (age 6)

Relational

Spreading rumors, ostracizing or exclusionary behaviors

My wife and I just went through a sticky divorce, and I got sole custody of our three children. We moved a short distance from our home. My daughter complained of stomach pains and didn't want to go to school. I thought she just missed her mom, but she finally told me that her classmates were avoiding her like the plague because someone started the rumor that her mother was unfit and didn't get custody because she was a drug-using prostitute.

—Martin, father of Karen (age 13)

Sexual

Inappropriate touching, threatening, or teasing that are sexually harassing

My daughter, Lynette, now refuses to wear some of her new, favorite school clothes. She finally confessed that she was ridiculed in school for her clothes being too revealing. One day during gym class, some of the other girls took her favorite (dry clean only) blouse and threw it in the showers to shrink it even more. They said they were tired of my daughter getting all of the attention from the boys.

—Tina, mother of Lynette (age 12)

Cyber

Bullying behaviors expressed through modern conveniences such as Internet chat rooms, hand-held walkie-talkies, and cellular phones

My son, Samuel, won't attend his physical education class anymore, and he is dangerously close to earning a failing grade. He finally confided that a classmate took his picture while showering using a picture phone. The student has placed his naked picture on the bathroom wall in school.

—Peter, father of Samuel (age 12)

Conflict

Conflict involves the opposition of two persons or things and is a naturally occurring human behavior that begins in early infancy and continues throughout the life span. Conflict is an essential component of all healthy relationships; experts note that either too little or too much conflict may signal a psychopathological relationship (Furman & Buhrmester, 1985).

Conflict and its constructive resolution often result in much cognitive and social growth and positive social interactions. Children who exhibit better problem-solving methods during conflict situations tend to enjoy healthier relationships with their peers than children who use destructive methods of resolving conflict (for example, physical fighting).

For example, two friends, Andy and Philip, need to select one topic for a class project, but they both have very different ideas. Andy wants to do the project on animals, while Philip wants to do the project on cars. Andy and Philip select the topic of stars, a topic that they both enjoy, and they complete the project successfully. Andy and Philip's experience with each other reinforces the use of collaboration as a conflict resolution technique and also establishes a beginning point of positive interactions between the two.

On the other hand, Philip could have given in to Andy and completed the project on animals. The conflict resolution strategy of giving in to Andy would have established an inequality in the relationship, whereby Philip might not have been interested in continuing a relationship. In many cases, conflict resolution strategy selection sets the tone of relationships for children. Collaborative strategies indicate more positive, longer-term friendships, and destructive strategies more often result in negative, shorter-term interactions between children.

Bully-victim relationships fit well within this depiction of conflict and aggression. As bullies and victims conflict over differences resulting from perceived or real power or hierarchy, it is most likely that they will use competitive methods of conflict resolution, not collaborative ones. Bully-victim relationships will involve short-term, negative conflicts in which participants use strategies such as aggression, giving in, or withdrawing to resolve the conflict. Bullies often choose aggressive methods of conflict resolution, while their victims often use avoidance strategies.

Witnesses in the middle school years tend not to become involved in the bullying episodes because of their concern with issues such as power and hierarchy. Becoming involved in bullying situations may jeopardize the tenuous balance of friendship patterns, which play such a significant role in socioemotional development during early adolescence.

Aggression

Although conflict and its resolution may occur with or without aggression, aggression usually does not occur without conflict. *Aggression* is defined as any behavior that results in physical or emotional injury to a person or animal, or one that leads to property damage or destruction. It can be verbal or physical. Not all forms of aggression are considered bullying behaviors.

Children engage in a number of different types of aggression that aren't necessarily bullying behaviors. Four different types of aggression that children express have been identified: accidental, expressive, instrumental, and hostile.

THE BULLY-VICTIM-WITNESS RELATIONSHIP

Bullying behaviors seldom occur in isolation. In fact, bullying frequently involves the support of peers within the school and is not an isolated event between two individuals.

According to one study, more than 85 percent of all bullying occurs within the context of peer group interactions (Atlas & Pepler, 1998). Although studies on bullying show that most children dislike bullying behaviors (Rigby & Slee, 1991), with 83 percent of youth reporting discomfort while watching these episodes (Craig & Pepler, 1997), bullies usually can find allies who share a dislike for victimized peers. Victims often perceive bystanders—or witnesses—as acting in collusion with the bullies. Some researchers suggest that 87 percent of all students may be identified as part of a bullying episode as a bully, victim, or witness (Huttunen et al., 1996).

Recent research in the fields of psychology and education has explored the relationship between bullies and their victims. Much has been written identifying characteristics of bully and victim, the origins of bullying and victim behaviors, and strategies for diminishing aggressive behavior in bullies and developing assertive skills among victims. However, much of this work has viewed the bully and the victim in isolation rather than as part of an interconnected, almost symbiotic relationship, whereby one would not exist without the other. Indeed, the bully-victim relationship is often composed of multiplayer interactions and is further complicated by influences such as other peers (witnesses), school personnel, and the children's families.

> Victims often perceive bystanders—or witnesses—as acting in collusion with the bullies. Some researchers suggest that 87 percent of all students may be identified as part of a bullying episode as a bully, victim, or witness.

Bully-victim-witness relationships must be viewed within a bidirectional context. Thus, bullies impact behaviors and thoughts of victims; conversely, victims impact behaviors and thoughts of their bullies in a bidirectional fashion. For example, the bully may attack, unnecessarily push, and shove his victim for playing poorly during a football game.

The victim, afraid and injured by the aggression, becomes more timid while playing, influencing greater physical aggression by the bully in response to the victim's poor athletic performance. This is not to suggest that victims of bullying deserve the bullying, but rather to demonstrate that bully-victim relationships depend on characteristic behaviors of both relationship partners. Compounding the situation, influences from other individuals, such as school personnel, family, and peers (witnesses), also impact the quality of the relationship between bullies and their victims.

Although this point is intuitive, remember that the context of the relationship is important before highlighting prevention and intervention strategies. Each member of the relationship plays a role in whether an interaction is positive or negative. Therefore, during a bullying episode, several individuals are involved, not just the bully and victim. Too often, prevention and intervention strategies focus only on changing the behavior of the bully.

Yet it is the bully-victim-witness relationship that must also change. Specific support and intervention must occur for bullies, victims, and witnesses in order to reduce bullying behaviors in schools. Developing and implementing a cookie-cutter approach to reducing bullying behaviors will not result in positive interactions among the participants in the future. It is not effective to target intentional aggression by bullies without focusing on victim behavior as well. Therefore, developing and implementing the prevention and intervention plan requires a conscious effort to target the context of the relationship and its multicomponents.

Types of Witnesses

As depicted in Figure 1.2, the bully-victim relationship involves more than the bully and the victim. These relationships include witnesses to the bully and the victim. Witnesses may take a number of roles within the bully-victim relationship.

Adults

School personnel and family members play a role in the bully-victim-witness relationship. School personnel may have a direct influence on the reduction of bullying behaviors, or, in contrast, may do much to reinforce or even escalate the bullying. School personnel may also influence the existence of interveners within the bullying relationship by encouraging their supportive nature.

Family members also play a significant role in this complex relationship. Modeling bullying or victim behaviors may reinforce children's expression of similar behaviors. Family members can also reinforce or discourage interveners through reward or punishment of the intervention, depending upon their perceptions of such bully-victim relationships. Family and school factors are discussed further in the next chapter.

Figure 1.2   The Bully-Victim-Witness Relationship

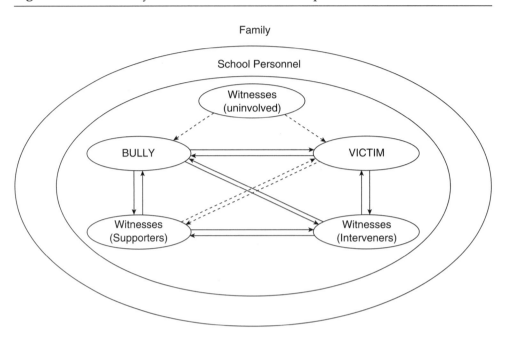

Bully Supporters

First, bully supporters are children who are witnesses to the bully-victim relationship and often incite the bully to participate in bullying behaviors without personally taking action against the victim. Generally, they do not interact with the victim. Instead, bully supporters increase the bullying behavior by creating a supportive environment for the bully; hence, the bully and supporter directly influence each other in the relationship, and this relationship indirectly influences the victim. The supporters' behaviors are often influenced by the bully's appreciation of their support and by the continued suffering of the victim. Males are more likely than females to be drawn into supporting the bullying behavior (Salmivalli, Lagerspetz, Bjorkqvist, Österman, & Kaukianinen, 1996).

Michael

Michael considers himself to be a "leader." At school he has a group of friends who are very popular. Michael and his friends meet in front of the school each morning. They stand near the sidewalk in a group, where they can make comments as certain students arrive at school. There are students whom they always target with insults. Sometimes they throw things at the target students and even push them. They like to knock one another around and purposefully collide with the student they are picking on.

Michael actively enjoys watching this bullying. He often just stands back and laughs as his friends make life miserable for other students. Sometimes his friends get in trouble with a teacher and are sent to the office. But they never tell the teacher or the principal that Michael is really the one who gets things going and eggs everyone on.

Interveners

Another form of witness is bully intervener—a child who intervenes on behalf of the victim during bullying situations. These witnesses are likely to stick up for the victim during bullying situations, or to console the victim following a bullying episode. Interveners are often motivated to defend or console victims not out of friendship with the victim but out of a sense of injustice and a desire to oppose the bullies and their supporters. The bullying behavior itself seems to reinforce the intervener's desire to intercede more than the victim's behavior does. According to Craig and Pepler (1997), peers intervened in 11 percent of playground bullying episodes; adults were significantly less likely to intervene, taking action only 4 percent of the time.

Meredith

Meredith is playing on the playground with her two friends. Suddenly she hears a low wailing coming from the enclosed playhouse. She sees a group of girls surrounding the new student. Meredith can just barely hear what they are saying to her, and it isn't nice. She is tired of the group ganging up on the "new kid" and decides that today is the day she is going to intervene. Meredith walks up to the group, and says in a loud voice, "This is stupid. I am sick of seeing you doing this to someone new all the time. Get a life!" The group is shocked.

Passive Supporters

Finally, bully-victim-witness relationships often include witnesses who are uninvolved with the bullying interaction. Victims and bullies often perceive these children as supporters of the act because they are passively involved and do not actively intervene in the situation. They indirectly influence the bully-victim relationships.

Marcia

Marcia has a few close friends at school but is more popular with girls from her neighborhood. Every day, Marcia watches Michael bullying other students as they enter the school. Marcia thinks that Michael is really cruel, as he often picks on special education students. Marcia would like to intervene, but she has never done it before, and she is afraid of the repercussions.

Types of Bullies

According to researchers, bullying behavior takes many forms, and children who participate in bullying behaviors often take different roles within the bully-victim relationship. For example, some witnesses may serve in supportive roles in the bullying relationship.

In general, two types of bullies exist. Bullies are categorized by (1) the level of conflict they engage in, and (2) the effectiveness of their aggression against victims. Figure 1.3 highlights these two categories, the bully (effectual) and bully-victim (ineffectual) types.

Effectual Bullies

Bullying encompasses a range of behaviors exhibited with varying degrees of success. Some bullies engage in few conflicts, yet are highly aggressive during conflict situations and tend to resolve the conflict on their terms. While in conflict, these bullies, called "effectual bullies," swiftly deal with their conflict partners. Usually these bullies deal unemotionally with their victims and very quickly move on following the conflict. Effectual bullies are more likely to initiate and actively play a role in

Figure 1.3   Levels of Conflict and Effectiveness in the Bully-Victim Relationship

Role	Level of Conflict	Bullying Effectiveness
BULLY	LOW	HIGH
BULLY-VICTIM	HIGH	LOW
VICTIM	LOW	LOW

the bullying episode. They usually encounter little resistance from their victims. Bullies tend to be somewhat unpopular but, unlike victims, may be popular with a particular group of children (Olweus, 1997).

This type of bully is the most common form and is the one most people think of when asked to describe bullying behavior.

Marcus

Marcus is tall for his age and is very strong. He likes to play on the baseball field at recess and rarely allows anyone outside of his peer group to play on the field at the same time. Daniel, a younger student, has been playing near the third baseline for the fourth day in a row. Marcus had spoken to him before playing on his field, but it appears that Daniel isn't heeding his warning. Looks like Daniel is going to be Marcus's newest victim.

Ineffectual Bullies

However, some bullies are often unsuccessful in their bullying behaviors. Ineffectual bullies frequently participate in conflict, yet are often not effective in asserting their aggression. Unlike effectual bullies, ineffectual bullies do not carry out the bullying behaviors using swift, unemotional methods. Instead, they continue to "jab" at the victim, who may or may not resist. Ineffectual bullies are often not successful in bullying their victims and often are at risk of becoming victims themselves.

Steven

Steven is very unpopular in school. He often gets into fights with other students and spends a great deal of time in detention. Steven is known by some students as a bully. He frequently starts his day by name calling, shoving, and threatening to "get" several students—all by 9:00 a.m.! One day, Steven went too far with a fellow student and was physically assaulted after calling the student a "loser."

Although it is unclear to researchers why these children engage in this behavior, some suggest that ineffectual bullies were bullied themselves and then model these methods with other children. Others suggest that these bullies actually began as bullies, were ineffective in their methods, and became victimized as a result. Often these ineffectual bullies play the role of the bully supporter in order to be provided with opportunities to succeed in bullying vicariously through the effectual bully. Ineffectual bullies are just as likely, however, to serve as the principal bully with additional ineffectual bullies serving as supporters.

Effectual bullies and ineffectual bullies differ according to their levels of peer popularity, which also support the demonstration of their bullying behavior. Effectual bullies are more popular among their peers as compared to ineffectual bullies, who demonstrate negative personality characteristics and are more disliked by peers (Pelligrini, 1998).

Types of Victims

In comparison to bullies, little research has been conducted into the backgrounds and behavior of children who serve as the victims in bully-victim relationships. Some researchers do suggest, however, that victims are often more similar to bullies in methods of problem solving than not, particularly with regard to conflict behavior. Both victims and bullies use competitive forms of conflict resolution, with victimized children often resolving conflict through avoidance and bullies through aggressive means. As a group, victims cry easily, are disliked by peers, and are anxious and lonely (Olweus, 1978; Schwartz, Dodge, & Coie, 1993). Similar to bullies, victims can be categorized according to the level of conflict in which they are involved.

High-Conflict Victims

Some victimized children engage in high levels of conflict. Victims who engage in high levels of conflict are often aggressive, yet unsuccessful in "winning" conflicts with others. Also referred to as "provocative" or "aggressive" victims, 10–20 percent of victims are bullies as well (Olweus, 2001). These children often exhibit behaviors that are highly irritating, such as disruptiveness, hyperactivity, and aggression. For instance, high-conflict victims will frequently provoke other children and will respond aggressively when provoked. These children will lose many of their battles while displaying great frustration and bitterness. They are at great risk for serving as victims in bullying-victim relationships. Often high-conflict victims are also ineffectual bullies.

Milton

Teachers are always having to remind Milton to sit in his chair to finish a lesson. He frequently picks on other students in class. One day, Milton made animal sounds when the teacher called on a particular student. Milton's frequent target was absent from school another day, and Milton attempted to bully the student's "backup," when suddenly, Milton was victimized by another student!

Low-Conflict Victims

On the other hand, low-conflict victims do not demonstrate aggressive behaviors, but rather are passive and submissive when confronted in bullying episodes. These children yield submissively and quickly to the demands of an aggressor, ending the conflict. Therefore, conflicts do not occur over extended periods of time.

Pierce (1990), as cited in Perry, Perry, and Kennedy (1992), found that high-conflict victims were more disliked by their peers than were low-conflict victims. High-conflict victims were more likely to be described as always needing to have their own way, ready to blame others, argumentative, disruptive, and persistent in attempts to enter peer groups. In contrast, low-conflict victims are more likely to be described by peers as withdrawn and reluctant to interact with peers.

Interestingly, parental involvement is correlated to victimization. Children who are more likely to become victimized tend to have involved parents. Again, it is unclear if parents become more involved in response to bullying behaviors against their child, or if their involvement indicates their difficulty in allowing their children to function independently.

Angela

Angela has two very good friends at school, but generally she keeps to herself. She is quite self-conscious about her appearance and does not like having to change clothes for physical education. The school bully has targeted her during the last month and is becoming increasingly threatening. Today, the bully has demanded that Angela hand over a favorite necklace that she was storing in her gym locker.

RESEARCH FINDINGS ON BULLIES AND VICTIMS

Researchers have attempted to identify trends with regard to bullying behaviors in order to understand the nature of bullies and their victims. Trends have emerged identifying differences in gender, age, and ethnicity. Although many of these studies were conducted in countries outside of the United States, they still provide useful information for American educators and parents.

Gender Differences

Researchers suggested that gender differences are apparent with regard to bullying behavior. Specifically, gender is related to the demonstration of bullying behavior and methods of bullying. Olweus (1978) noted that males are more likely to demonstrate bullying behaviors through physical violence and aggression or threat of physical violence or aggression. Females, on the other hand, more frequently use indirect or relational modes of bullying, such as gossiping, spreading rumors, and ostracizing (Bjorkqvist, Lagerspetz, & Kaukianinen, 1992; Rivers & Smith, 1994).

Gender differences also are evident in victim selection. Males are equally likely to bully males and females, while females almost exclusively bully other females. Males are more likely to bully than females in a 3:1 ratio and will bully children from other grades in the school. Females are less likely to bully than males, and females tend to choose their victims from their own grade.

Although females are reported to bully less frequently than males, documented cases may not clearly represent the true incidence, since girls use more covert methods of bullying behavior than males and are underrepresented in the literature. Also, bullying behavior among males may be overrepresented if self-reporting measures are used because male bullying behaviors are more socially acceptable than female forms of bullying. Therefore, males might be more willing to admit their bullying behavior than females. One possible reason for bullying differences between males and females is their different motives. While males tend to bully to demonstrate power and hierarchy, girls demonstrate bullying behaviors for reassurance or affiliation (Wachtel, 1973). On self-report surveys, males and females are equally likely to report being victimized (Charach, Pepler, & Ziegler, 1995).

> Males are more likely to bully than females in a 3:1 ratio and will bully children from other grades in the school. Females are less likely to bully than males, and females tend to choose their victims from their own grade.

Age Differences

Age differences have been found in bullying studies in Scandinavian countries, with some preliminary evidence in America supporting these findings. Olweus (1996) found significant differences with regard to age in identifying bully behavior in Europe. The incidence of bullying behavior is twice as high among elementary as in secondary school students; however, students transitioning from schools are at greatest risk for bullying behavior. Bullying behavior was at its highest rate among children in their final years of attendance at any particular school (for example, among sixth graders in a K–6 school and among twelfth graders in a traditional high school). Developmentally, girls' bullying behavior declines over the years, while males' bullying behavior tends to increase. Physical bullying decreases with age in both genders.

In the United States, bullying tends to increase during the late elementary years, peaking during the middle school grades. Espelage and Holt (2001) found that after the transition to middle school, the sixth graders reported more use of teasing and bullying behaviors than elementary grades. Bullying decreases after the ninth grade, when children reach

> Bullying behavior was at its highest rate among children in their final years of attendance at any particular school (for example, among sixth graders in a K–6 school and among twelfth graders in a traditional high school).

approximately 14 years of age (Hazler, Carney, Green, Powell, & Jolly, 1997). Therefore, youth in Grades 6–8 are at greatest risk for experiencing bullying behaviors. Some researchers also suggest that bullying may be a way to establish dominance in social structures, and therefore, the transition to middle school will likely be accompanied by an increase in bullying and then followed by an age-related decline in high school as dominance hierarchies are solidified (Pelligrini & Long, 2002).

Indeed, this overlaps well with reported elevated levels of conflict—both peer conflict and familial conflict—that occur among this age group. In the United States, this age group is often reported to demonstrate the highest levels of risk-taking behaviors (for example, smoking, drug use, sexual activity). Olweus (1993) reported that children in lower grades are more likely to be victims of older bullies, whereas children in upper grades are more likely to be victims of same-age bullies. Smith and Shu (2000) found that older children were more likely than younger children to report using effective strategies against bullies.

Ethnic Differences

Although the literature is scant, ethnicity and race do seem to influence the risk of participating in bully-victim relationships. White, non-Hispanic students are more likely than Black, non-Hispanic students to report being bullied. White and Black students report greater incidence of indirect or relational bullying as compared to Hispanic students. White students were more likely than Black students to report being bullied (Hanish & Guerra, 2000).

Rigby (1998) described bullies as possessing strong racist attitudes. Often, children of the minority group in a classroom are victims, and they tend to view their peers' aggression as bullying rather than racism. These findings are certainly consistent, as children are more likely to initiate isolation and separation based upon differences at this age than during other developmental periods.

In preliminary findings, Barton (2000) found bullying behaviors were reported more frequently in diverse school communities as compared to more homogeneous school populations.

Socioeconomic Status

Olweus (1980) found no relationship between socioeconomic status of the family and being the victim of bullying and indicates that there are similar proportions of bullies and victims across all levels. Olweus attributes this finding, however, to the relative homogeneity in the Scandinavian countries in which his studies were conducted. DeVoe and Kaffenberger (2005) found similar results in the United States; however, additional research must be conducted.

Bullying and Special Student Populations

Very little research has been conducted on bullying and special populations of students. The limited research on bullying in special education has indicated that special education students are more likely to be victimized (Llewellyn, 2000). The scant research of bullying among children with learning disabilities suggests that they are vulnerable to being victimized, as these students are at risk for being rejected and unpopular with peers.

Effects of the Bully-Victim-Witness Relationships

Researchers have identified both long-term and short-term effects of the bully-victim-witness relationship. However, these effects cannot be generalized as the type of bully and type of victim affect these findings. Carefully designed empirical studies using a longitudinal design (studying the same individuals over an extended period of time) are necessary to identify clear psychosocial correlates of this relationship.

Effect on Bullies

Much has been written about both the short-term and long-term impact of bullying behaviors. According to a study in the *Journal of the American Medical Association* (Nansel, Overpeck et al., 2001), bullies are more likely than other children to be involved with risk-taking and problem behaviors such as drinking alcohol and smoking. Bullies are more likely to demonstrate antisocial and rule-breaking behaviors such as with vandalism, truancy, and frequent drug use. According to Berthold and Hover (2000), middle school bullies were more likely to be pressured by peers into high-risk behaviors such as smoking and drinking. Bullies also demonstrated poorer school adjustment, including lower academic achievement and a more negative perception of the school climate. Interestingly, the social and psychological maladjustment associated with relational bullying is as significant and stable as those of physical bullying (Galen & Underwood, 1997).

Researchers disagree, however, regarding the impact of bullying on social behavior. Bjorkqvist, Ekman, and Lagerspetz (1982) found bullies to be unpopular among peers, but not as unpopular as their victims. Bullies, according to self-reports, perceive themselves as impulsive and lacking in self-control (Bjorkqvist et al., 1992) and tend to be attracted to social situations with aggressive content. Olweus (1992) found bullies were four times more likely to be involved with criminal behaviors at the age of 24, with 60 percent demonstrating at least one conviction and 35–40 percent showing three or more convictions.

Eron, Huesmann, Dubow, Romanoff, and Yarmel (1987) found that those who were labeled as bullies by their classmates remained bullies throughout their lives; they accumulated more court convictions, experienced more alcoholism and antisocial personality disorders, and used more mental health services than their peers.

However, bullies are less likely to experience negative consequences as compared to individuals who participate as both bullies and victims. According to the *Journal of the American Medical Association* (Nansel, Overpeck, et al., 2001) study, children who serve as both bully and victim demonstrate poorer adjustment across socioemotional dimensions.

Effect on Victims

Victims who participate in low levels of conflict tend to demonstrate poorer social and emotional adjustment than nonvictims. As children, victims tend to have greater difficulty making friends with same-age peers; they demonstrate poorer quality interactions with classmates, and report greater loneliness than nonvictims. Victims also demonstrate poorer problem-solving skills than nonvictimized youth; however, it is unknown if this is a result of the bullying behavior or an underlying cause of the behavior. Victims report low self-esteem, likely because of repeated exposure to victimization (Besag, 1989). Depression and loss of interest in activities are common (Craig & Pepler, 1997), as are anxiety, tension, and fear (Slee, 1995). As a result of bullying, suicidal ideation is high among victimized children (Carney, 2000; National Center for Education Statistics, 1995).

> Bullies were four times more likely to be involved with criminal behavior at the age of 24, with 60 percent demonstrating one conviction and 35–40 percent showing three or more convictions.

Long-term effects of victimization are evident. Individuals formerly bullied were found to have higher levels of depression and poorer self-esteem at age 23, and they were more harassed and socially isolated than comparison adults (Olweus, 1994). This may result from an internalization of perceptions that they are worthless or inadequate.

Farrington (1991) cited that victims are less likely to be involved with delinquent behaviors than are bullies.

SUMMARY

As educators and parents, we must appreciate the complexities of the bully-victim-witness relationship if we hope to change it. Bullying is intentional, repeated aggression within an interpersonal relationship characterized by a real or perceived imbalance of power. What does bullying look like? Most of us picture physical aggression when we think of bullying, but bullying may take the more subtle forms of teasing or gossip. The power bullies wield may be based on their physical size or on less tangible factors such as their popularity with peers. Finally, bullying often is a three-way relationship in which bystanders have the power to intervene or support the behavior.

Bullying has significant short-term and long-term results. Parents and educators should be aware that bullies tend to engage in more risk-taking behaviors than their peers, while victims have a harder time adjusting socially and forming same-age friendships. In later life, bullies tend to adjust poorly, with a far greater incidence of emotional problems and criminal behavior. Their victims also experience long-term effects, most notably higher rates of depression and suicidal ideation.

The stakes are high, therefore, for both bullies and victims. Understanding and influencing bullying behavior provides educators and parents with a significant opportunity to have a profound impact on the quality of children's lives and futures.

2

Origins of Bully-Victim-Witness Behavior

Explaining the possible origins of bully-victim relationships is an important step in preventing bullying relationships in the school setting. Psychologists often attempt to explain children's physical, cognitive, and social development based on genetic or environmental influences. For instance, researchers have long been interested in explaining the source of children's intelligence and how genetics or environment might influence it. Child-rearing practices and their relationship to school achievement are also a question of nature versus nurture. Although no single influence definitively explains bullying behavior, the age-old argument of nature (genetic contribution) versus nurture (environmental contribution) in the psychological field is certainly one place to begin in an attempt to understand the origins of bully-victim-witness behaviors.

NATURE VERSUS NURTURE

Nature may play a role in bullying. For example, males more frequently demonstrate bullying behaviors, such as physical aggression, than females. Nature advocates might hypothesize, therefore, that increased levels of testosterone predispose men to demonstrate more physical bullying behaviors than women. Perhaps low hormonal levels in children may be linked to nonaggressive means of conflict resolution. Furthermore, parents who engage in bullying behaviors and whose children demonstrate similar bullying behaviors support the theory of a genetic component to bullying. Theories abound regarding the link between nature and behavior.

Yet, bullying and victimization behaviors may be the result of nurture, or the environment in which the child has been raised, rather than the product of genetics. Perhaps the parents or guardians clearly demonstrate victimization or bullying behaviors in their interpersonal relationships, creating a model for the child's behavior. Do media sources, such as television and/or videos, depict males as more aggressive bullies than females, perhaps modeling bullying for males? Additional research needs to be done to answer important questions:

- Why do children behave as bullies, victims, and/or witnesses?
- Where do these behaviors come from?
- Are these behaviors sustainable and generalizable to other relationships?

FAMILY CHARACTERISTICS

Researchers have identified significant trends in family characteristics as they relate to bullies and their victims. Families of bullies have in the home a high degree of conflict that often includes violence (Olweus, 1997), a lack of warmth and involvement, and inadequate limits. Rather than providing children with structure and developmentally appropriate guidelines with high warmth, parents of bullies often demonstrate highly authoritarian or permissive parenting strategies. In fact, parents who rule their children with an iron fist offer their children few decision-making opportunities, resulting in children who are at higher risk for succumbing to peer influence and developing victimization behaviors. Parents of children who engage in relational bullying may invalidate their child's feelings, threaten to withdraw love affection, or use sarcasm and power-assertive methods of discipline (Maccoby & Martin, 1983). Nelson and Crick (2001) found that maternal coercive control and maternal corporal punishment were significantly associated with relational aggression for boys.

Parents who frequently fight in front of their children are more likely to have noncompliant and aggressive children at home and school than are more peaceful parents. A number of possible explanations exist to support this. First, parents who use destructive methods of conflict resolution are less likely to create secure attachments in children (Howes & Markman, 1989) and are less likely to manage sibling conflicts effectively (Patterson, 1982). Next, according to Bandura (1973), children may merely be modeling their parents' behavior during times of social conflict. Last, these parents may also produce children who are unable to regulate their emotions during conflicts (Cummings, Vogel, Cummings, & El-Sheikh, 1989). On the other hand, children who are able to soothe themselves during heightened emotional states are using a type of cognitive processing that inhibits an aggressive response. In addition, literature suggests that children's exposure to violence or experiences with violence in the home predisposes them to becoming perpetrators or victims of violence themselves.

Sibling relationships also serve as important socialization models for children's bullying behaviors. It is well established that physical aggression in sibling relationships has a strong influence on the acquisition and demonstration of aggressive behaviors (Patterson, 1986). Although not yet confirmed with research, it is likely that levels of bullying, especially relational bullying, in sibling relationships are most likely to play a role in levels of bullying behaviors exhibited in peer relationships, given that sibling interactions serve as a model for learning about social behaviors (Azmitia & Hesser, 1993).

INDIVIDUAL CHARACTERISTICS

In addition to coming from high-risk families, do children who demonstrate bullying or victimization behaviors possess certain individual characteristics that may place them at risk for participating in bully-victim relationships?

Personality Traits

Children who demonstrate aggressive behavior often have been studied for purposes of identifying specific personality traits and their relationship to behavior. The classic psychological work of Thomas and Chess (1977) in the field of temperament does shed some light on the connection between individual characteristics and the expression of bullying and victim behaviors. In this study, also known as the "New York Longitudinal Study," Thomas and Chess identified three styles of temperament—one's characteristic style of interacting with the world. Two of the three categories identified by Chess are relevant in discussing the connection between personalities and bullying behavior. They are the easy temperament child and the difficult temperament child.

Easy temperament children are highly social, slow to react negatively, and not easily agitated. When agitated, easy temperament children quickly adapt to the new situation and are easily consoled. On the other hand, difficult temperament children are more likely to be highly irritable, easily agitated, and highly reactive. Difficult temperament children are unable to transition quickly when presented with a new situation. Difficult temperament children are more at risk for insecure attachments than are children with easy temperaments. Therefore, difficult temperament children are more likely to demonstrate behaviors consistent with high-conflict ineffectual bullies, while easy temperament children are more likely not to be involved in bully-victim relationships.

Sociocognitive Skills

Children's sociocognitive skills, or their ability to process and think about social situations, must also be included as a possible explanation for bullying or victimization behaviors. Specifically, researchers have considered how children's sociocognitive skills, or skills in "theory of mind," affect how well they understand the mental states, beliefs, and emotions of others. Intuitively, one may speculate that children with sophisticated sociocognitive skills would not be involved with bullying behaviors because they would understand the anxiety, frustration, and hurt caused to another person through their actions. Children with less sophisticated skills would be less empathetic and hence more likely to demonstrate bullying behaviors.

Researchers, however, have not supported the picture of bullies who are physically powerful but cognitively unsophisticated. Rather, some bullies actually demonstrate a highly sophisticated understanding of other people's perspectives. Sutton, Smith, Smith, and Swettenham (1999) suggest that different types of bullies (ringleaders versus followers) possess differing abilities when it comes to appreciating the viewpoints of others. Rather than the stereotype that "all bullies lack empathy," Sutton suggests that ringleader types of bullies possess highly advanced abilities to appreciate the perspectives of others, while followers do not. Females, who participate in relational bullying more often than males, also possess highly sophisticated sociocognitive skills. Sutton et al. (1999) suggest that, in some cases, these females use their sociocognitive abilities as a tool to further isolate and ostracize victims.

Children may possess sophisticated sociocognitive skills but may not use these skills in interpersonal relationships. Specifically, children may demonstrate skill and performance differences in taking the perspective of others in bully-victim-witness relationships. This is particularly important when implementing anti-bullying initiatives, as sociocognitive training programs must address both skills and performance of these skills in social situations.

Although additional research must be conducted in this area, it may be hypothesized that bullies possess sophisticated sociocognitive skills (as evidenced by their ferocious intimidation techniques) yet fail to use these skills in positive ways. Similarly, victims are likely to possess highly sophisticated sociocognitive skills, but performance of these skills is low. On the other hand, the child who is both the bully and the victim potentially possesses both low sociocognitive skills and low performance of those skills in social situations. School leaders should not be concerned with "improving" the negative sociocognitive skills of bullies with the implementation of anti-bullying initiatives. Rather, the anti-bullying initiatives should include developing all students' sociocognitive skills and their constructive use.

Frustration-Aggression Theory

Another common explanation of bullying behaviors is that children who bully are more likely encountering frustration with schoolwork. Frustration-aggression theory explains that bullies demonstrate the negative behavior as a result of being frustrated with failures (either academic or social). Olweus (1983) found, however, that although an association exists between aggressive behavior and poor grades, there is no direct evidence that aggressive behavior is a consequence of poor grades and failure in school.

Social Support

Social support is defined as a set of perceived general or specific supportive behaviors that contribute to a person's physical and mental well-being and can serve as a buffer for someone under stress (Malecki & Demaray, 2002). Having low levels of perceived social support can be related to a variety of poor psychological (Compas, Slavin, Wagner, & Vannatta, 1986), social (Bender & Losel, 1997), academic (Malecki & Demaray, 2002), and physical (Frey & Rothlisberger, 1996) outcomes. Rigby (2000) identified that victims of bullying were more likely to perceive lower levels of social support from classmates. Furthermore, Rigby found that frequency of being victimized and low social support were significant contributors to students' general health, including somatic, anxiety, social functioning, and depressive symptoms.

Victims are more likely to rate social support as more important than are bullies, regardless of the source of the support (for example, parents, peers, or teachers). Teachers contribute to bullying behaviors, as bullies may be more difficult in the classroom and frustrating for teachers. Malecki and Demaray (2003) found that bullies perceived significantly less social support than nonbullies. Given these results, one possible intervention is helping teachers find ways to begin or continue to provide social support to bullies in their classrooms.

Both bullies and victims benefit from support services (for example, social support groups, skills groups) in school, where they can learn to cope with victimization, learn constructive means of conflict resolution, and assist in setting up proactive plans that reduce opportunities for destructive interpersonal interactions. Researchers suggest that high levels of social support, such as close friendships, buffer children from negative outcomes of victimization (Prinstein, Boergers, & Vernberg, 2001). Thus, promoting positive peer relationships is an important area of intervention.

SCHOOL AND CLASSROOM CHARACTERISTICS

School and classroom characteristics are important to consider in explaining bullying behaviors. According to DeVoe and Kaffenberger (2005), fewer students reported bullying in schools where there was supervision by police officers, security officers, or staff hallway monitors. Students in schools with hallway monitors reported less victimization than students in schools without the staff support (14 percent versus 18 percent). In addition, students in schools where gangs were present were more likely to report being the victims of bullying than students in schools that reported no presence of street gangs.

Literature on bullying and school violence points to classroom and school environments playing roles in the maintenance of students' aggressive behaviors (Barth, Dane, Dunlap, Lochman, & Wells, 2001; Song & Swearer, 2002). Many schools have an unofficial reputation among students for tolerating bullying behavior. School administrators may be lenient with students who are habitually involved with bullying behaviors, or ignore incidents, particularly relational bullying behaviors such as gossip or rumors. Jeffrey, Miller, and Linn (2001) stated that a general attitude among teachers and school administrators has been that meanness is a normative developmental feature of middle school students. As a result, students may perceive the school as unsafe and be reluctant or unwilling to notify school faculty and administration of bullying behaviors. The lack of strong support against bullying behaviors establishes an environment that consistently reinforces the individual roles of bully supporters and bystanders. Students who might otherwise serve as victim interveners may hesitate to assist the victim because the school administrators choose not to be involved. Bully supporters may continue to reinforce the bullying behaviors if they go relatively unpunished by administration, and, finally, bystanders may choose to remain passively involved in bullying episodes, quickly modeling the lack of support from the administration.

Teacher Training

One reason many students may perceive their schools as unsafe is that the teaching faculty may be unprepared for handling bully-victim relationships. Researchers have identified that teachers often underestimate the prevalence of bullying in their schools (Smith & Sharp, 1994). O'Moore, Kirkham, and Smith (1997) found that 27 percent of primary teachers and 53 percent of secondary teachers in Ireland did not recognize bullying as a problem in their schools. As well, teachers lacked sufficient knowledge regarding bullying and methods for intervening in bullying episodes. Hazler, Carney, Green, Powell, and Jolly (1997) suggest that teachers may have difficulty discriminating among bullying, teasing, victimization, and play. Craig, Henderson, and Murphy (2000) found that prospective teachers were less likely to identify social isolation as bullying behavior, and tended to feel that physical bullying behavior was the most severe and most warranted intervention, as compared to emotional and/or verbal bullying behaviors. Specifically, teachers perceive relational bullying behaviors as less serious than verbal or physical bullying and are less likely to intervene (Craig et al., 2000).

Charach, Pepler, and Ziegler (1995) found that students do not believe that adults will respond effectively to bullying and therefore are less likely to report it. Olweus (1994) found that teachers intervene inconsistently and infrequently during bullying episodes. According to interview data (Simmons, 2002), students reported that teachers are either unaware of what is going on in their classrooms or uninvolved in helping students have better social experiences. Researchers found that factors related to teachers, including witnessing the interaction and possessing a level of empathy, were predictors of intolerant attitudes toward bullying (Craig et al., 2000). Unfortunately, teachers' mishandling and lack of involvement in bullying behaviors can be interpreted as condoning the behaviors, thereby creating a hidden curriculum that reinforces bullying (Yoon & Kerber, 2003).

Social Climate

Levels of bully-victim relationships in schools are connected to the social climate of the school or classroom involved. In schools or classrooms where bullying occurs quite often, students tend to feel less safe and less satisfied with school life. Persistent bullying behaviors that remain unchecked by teaching faculty or administrators greatly affect the bully, the victim, and witnesses. When victims of bullying perceive their plight as going unnoticed, they are less likely to feel safe in their school environment (Yoon & Kerber, 2003). Unpunished acts teach witnesses that bullying behaviors are acceptable; victims remain victimized, and the climate becomes one lacking in empathy. In contrast, positive school climates that adopt punitive policies toward bullying behaviors with clear consequences for such behaviors create more positive attitudes in students regarding bully-victim relationships. A lack of policies and procedures outlining consequences for bullying behavior invites and validates bullying behaviors in the classroom, in hallways, and on the playground.

Class Size

Contradictory evidence exists as to a relationship between school and classroom size and bullying behaviors. O'Moore et al. (1997) found an inverse relationship between the size of the class and school and the level of bullying behaviors reported. In this study, children attending small schools and smaller classrooms experienced fewer bullying behaviors. Olweus (1993) found, however, that the size of the classroom and school had a negligible effect on the relative frequency of bully-victim behaviors in a school. Whitney and Smith (1993) reported no relationship between school bullying and school size.

Bullying on the Playground

Bullying is affected, however, by the amount of structure provided during free periods. Bullying behaviors often occur on playgrounds, at break times, or at lunchtime (Ross & Ryan, 1990; Whitney & Smith, 1993). Whitney and Smith (1993) studied 24 schools in Sheffield, England, and showed that the playground was the most frequent place for bullying to occur, especially in the elementary grades. One of the reasons, they suggest, is ineffective supervision. Other reasons included boredom, overcrowding, and opportunities for exclusion. The physical environment of the playground influences many of these factors.

Higgins (1994) stated that overcrowding on playgrounds may incite bullying, particularly if the school grounds are large, featureless, unstructured spaces where children are forced to compete for space and scant resources. Such spaces lend themselves to chasing or running games. These overcrowded, unstructured spaces are unlikely to stimulate children's interests, producing boredom, frustration, and, in turn, bullying.

Unstructured playground areas will emphasize running games such as football or tag, with much of the space taken by teams, primarily males. Segregation of some males and females to the outside of the game areas is a common outcome in these playground settings. Children who do not excel in running games are pushed further toward the periphery of social interactions, both literally and figuratively. A playground that is good for running games but lacks resources and structure for other types of activities tends to reinforce certain social relationships. Playground environments establish that those who do not excel in running activities must be excluded and have little opportunity to excel due to the lack of alternative activities (Besag, 1991).

Adult supervision is the other important factor in playground bullying. One of the greatest correlates of increased bullying on the playground during lunchtime and breaks is lack of adult supervision. In some schools, problems may result from too few adults on the playground. Another issue may be inappropriately trained personnel supervising the playground. Figure 2.1 illustrates these different bullying risk factors. Methods for dealing with playground bullying are discussed in the next chapter, as part of the discussion of the anti-bullying component of the safe school plan.

Figure 2.1   Bullying Risk Factors

- Insecure attachment, resulting from inconsistent or authoritarian styles of parenting
- Parents who ineffectively manage both their own conflicts and conflicts with their children
- Lack of parental support and acceptance, which leads to a difficult temperament
- Lack of teacher training regarding bully prevention strategies
- Lack of policies and procedures outlining consequences for bullying behavior
- Inadequate structure and supervision during free periods, especially on the playground

SUMMARY

Researchers are still at work uncovering the origins of bullying and victim behaviors. Theories focus on both genetic input and environmental influences, the age-old debate between nature and nurture. Family characteristics, individual characteristics, and aspects of the school environment have all been examined in the effort to understand what creates bullies and their victims. Parents who fail to consistently and appropriately meet their children's need seem to place those children at risk for participation in bully-victim relationships. Schools that ineffectively manage bullying earn a reputation among the students for tolerating violence, contributing to the cycle of aggression and victimization.

Further work is necessary to pinpoint the exact sources of bullying, but families and schools can begin to take action now. Clearly, parents must provide positive role models for managing conflict; they must work from infancy on to meet their children's needs and thus make possible the development of empathy for others. Schools must train teachers to deal appropriately with bullying incidents rather than look the other way; they must establish policies and procedures outlining clear consequences for bullying behavior, and provide adequate adult supervision at all times so that those policies can be enforced. Together, families and schools can help reduce the incidence of bullying behavior and provide children with safe, secure neighborhoods and schools.

3

Implementing the Schoolwide Anti-Bullying Program

Many researchers contend that the hallmarks of American schools contribute to the isolation and segregation of students, thereby allowing bully-victim relationships to thrive. Aaron Kipnis (1999) argued that schools condone bullying, teasing, and cliques by dividing and labeling students according to their academic and athletic gifts. Sorting by ability strengthens the likelihood that some students will not be part of any crowd. Often, the school initiates these differences with clear delineation (for example, varsity letters, sports awards, academic honors), and students then do whatever it takes to continue these lines of separation and maintain their position within the school hierarchy. The middle school years are particularly pivotal for preventing bullying, as the routine and lack of differentiation in elementary school quickly gives way to opportunities to segregate and isolate.

Approaches to anti-bullying initiatives may be considered from the micro-level (classroom) to the macro-level (districtwide). Figure 3.1 provides examples of initiatives at both levels.

Figure 3.1   Levels of Anti-Bullying Initiatives

Districtwide Initiatives (Macro-Level)

- Policies and procedures
- District safety plans, including anti-bullying
- School- or buildingwide initiatives
- School safety plans
- Bullying assessment
- Staff development
- Programming initiatives
- Curriculum support
- Programming evaluation

Classroom Initiatives (Micro-Level)

- Bullying assessment
- Curriculum support
- Classroom ground rules

Districtwide activities that support anti-bullying may include:

- Developing policies and procedures outlining districtwide definitions and punitive or disciplinary measures
- Designing school safety plans that include anti-bullying initiatives to reduce youth violence and improve the learning environment

School districts should consider supporting efforts by implementing strong anti-bullying policies and procedures and by funding supportive educational programming. Districts with safe school plans may support anti-bullying initiatives with relatively little effort by inserting anti-bullying policies in their current school safety planning. Financial support for anti-bullying efforts may become part of a school district's overall violence prevention programming. Funding is often available through the federal Safe and Drug-Free Schools and Communities program and other Title I programs.

Although districtwide support of anti-bullying initiatives is preferable, it is not necessary for school-level programming success. Schools may develop effective anti-bullying efforts within the school building. With any schoolwide effort, a primary predictor of program success is the commitment and interest of school administration in changing the school climate. Without administrative support, anti-bullying efforts in the organization cannot be fully actualized.

ANTI-BULLYING PROGRAM DEVELOPMENT AND IMPLEMENTATION SAMPLE

Step 1: Preliminary Program Development

1. Establish an advisory committee to oversee the development of a school policy, administer the program, and help trouble-shoot and publicize the program. If the school currently has an active school safety team, the school may wish to develop a subcommittee of the school safety team for the anti-bullying program. If the school does not currently have a school safety team, the school should recruit parents, school administrators, faculty, and others. Research the anti-bullying policies and procedures of schools in the area.

2. Develop an anti-bullying program plan. The plan should include a timetable for the development of a school policy, implementation of professional development activities, imple-mentation of educational training programs for students, identi-fication of a time line for enforcement of new policy, and a timetable for the review and evaluation of the program.

3. Administer an anonymous survey to students assessing the extent to which bullying behaviors occur in the school. (See Figure 3.2 for a sample survey.) Students should complete the survey prior to the development of the school policy so that defined actions of bullying will be adequately addressed. The survey is critical in identifying a common understanding of the issue of bullying by students as well as providing baseline data on the extent of bullying in the school.

4. Administer an anonymous survey to school faculty to assess their perceptions of the extent to which bully-victim behaviors occur in the schools.

5. Using unsophisticated statistical analysis, compare and contrast student responses with school staff responses. Differences in perceptions of amount, type, and severity of bullying will help school safety members appreciate the importance of their mission. It is likely that teachers will report fewer, less severe incidents of bullying behaviors than students. Use of this data will assist the committee in devel-oping appropriate school policies.

6. Create policies and procedures associated with the anti-bullying program, using requirements of state legislation and

districtwide policies, results of surveys presented to staff and students, and resources available.

7. Present findings of the surveys at an all-staff inservice. Provide packets of information to school faculty on the consequences of bullying, long and short term, and ways to identify bullying behavior. Identify areas of the school that are most likely to support or facilitate bullying behavior. Create a timetable for professional development on issues of bullying management and prevention.

8. Provide an anti-bullying play or presentation to parents so that they are aware of programming initiatives.

Step 2: Program Implementation

9. If anti-bullying curriculum is to be used schoolwide, train identified individuals and be sure they understand their roles.

10. Assess students' preprogram skills, knowledge, and attitudes.

11. Provide professional development to staff on anti-bullying.

12. Have school faculty and students design posters, bulletin boards, and school policies regarding the anti-bullying message and promoting anti-bullying programming.

13. Present anti-bullying program and policy to students through school assemblies and classroom presentations.

14. Rigorously monitor anti-bullying efforts.

15. Provide parent education meetings to discuss parenting effects on bullying behaviors and general constructive conflict resolution measures.

16. Develop a system to reinforce prosocial behavior, especially witnesses that intervene in bullying situations.

Step 3: Evaluation of the Anti-Bullying Efforts

17. Assess postprogramming variables of students' skills, knowledge, and attitudes.

18. Collect measures of changes in discipline and conduct of students, including incident reports, suspensions, and if used as a means of discipline, mediation reports.

19. Review curriculum for continued use in the school.

20. Identify new staff members for training.

Figure 3.2   Survey of Bullying Behaviors—Secondary

SAMPLE SURVEY OF STUDENTS

We are interested in learning how you feel about your school. Please read each question and circle the answer that best describes how you feel most of the time. The survey is anonymous, so no one will know how you answer.

Teacher: _____

Grade: _____   Date: _____

1. I think that my school is safe.

1	2	3	4	5
Strongly disagree	Disagree	Somewhat agree	Agree	Strongly agree

2. I feel safe in my classroom.

1	2	3	4	5
Strongly disagree	Disagree	Somewhat agree	Agree	Strongly agree

3. I feel safe in the hallway.

1	2	3	4	5
Strongly disagree	Disagree	Somewhat agree	Agree	Strongly agree

4. I feel safe in the cafeteria.

1	2	3	4	5
Strongly disagree	Disagree	Somewhat agree	Agree	Strongly agree

5. I feel safe on the playground.

1	2	3	4	5
Strongly disagree	Disagree	Somewhat agree	Agree	Strongly agree

6. I see bullying in school.

1	2	3	4
Never	Sometimes (1–2 times/month)	Often (1–2 times/week)	Every day

7. I see bullying in my classroom.

1	2	3	4
Never	Sometimes	Often	Every day

8. I see bullying on the playground.

1	2	3	4
Never	Sometimes	Often	Every day

9. How do adults react to bullying?
   a. They do nothing.
   b. They stop the bullying and punish the bully.
   c. They stop the bullying and try to talk out a solution.
   d. They stop the bullying but then walk away.
   e. Other: _____

10. How do you react to bullying?
   a. I do nothing.
   b. I join in the bullying.
   c. I stop the bullying and try to talk out a solution.
   d. I stop the bullying but then walk away.
   e. Other: _____

(Continued)

Figure 3.2 (Continued)

---

11. How do you think adults should react to bullying?
    a. They should do nothing.
    b. They should stop the bullying and punish the bully.
    c. They should stop the bullying and try to talk out a solution.
    d. They should stop the bullying but then walk away.
    e. Other: _____

12. What are some things that will stop bullying in your school? (Circle as many answers as you wish.)
    a. Teach ways to handle bullying
    b. Have more adults on the playground, in the cafeteria, and in hallways
    c. Create strict punishments for bullying
    d. Talk about cooperation and bullying prevention
    e. Other: _____

13. What are things that you can do to stop bullying in your school? (Circle as many answers as you wish.)
    a. Stop bullies by helping the victim
    b. Tell adults when bullying occurs
    c. Don't encourage bullying by standing by or joining in the bullying
    d. Tell the bully to stop
    e. Other: _____

14. How often have you been bullied?

1	2	3	4
Never	Sometimes	Often	Every day

15. How often do you bully?

1	2	3	4
Never	Sometimes	Often	Every day

16. Bullying behaviors include the following: (Please circle all the items you agree with.)
    a. Teasing
    b. Hitting
    c. Harassing
    d. Gossiping
    e. Name calling
    f. Hazing
    g. Pinching
    h. Threatening

17. Where does bullying behavior most frequently occur?
    a. Classrooms
    b. Hallways
    c. Playground
    d. Cafeteria
    e. To and from school

DEVELOPMENT OF SCHOOLWIDE ANTI-BULLYING PROGRAMS

This section of the chapter identifies and explains the components of an effective anti-bullying program and the necessary steps for creating one. School change agents need to identify a projected time line for the anti-bullying campaign that includes preliminary program development, implementation, and the evaluation that is necessary for modifying program implementation in the future. A sample anti-bullying program is provided; however, each school will need to modify the time line depending on the goals (for example, comprehensiveness of scope) of its anti-bullying program.

Elements of a Schoolwide Anti-Bullying Initiative

Schools can do much to improve students' perceptions of the safety of the school and the level of tolerance demonstrated toward bully-victim-witness relationships. For schools in states with anti-bullying legislation, these voluntary measures will support the state and local legislative policies, thereby improving the safety of the school community.

Once school administrators and faculty commit to building a supportive, safer learning environment through strong anti-bullying messages, they must develop, implement, and modify supportive components of the anti-bullying plan. One of the most essential mechanisms for garnering school community support for anti-bullying initiatives is to convene a committee of individuals to assist in the initiative as members of an anti-bullying committee.

Creating the Anti-Bullying Committee

Before developing the schoolwide anti-bullying plan, schools will need to convene a group that will be responsible for developing the elements of the plan. School change agents such as school superintendents, the principal, or a designated agent within the school building should facilitate the process of building a team to identify issues of school safety, one issue being anti-bullying policies and programming. Most schools with an established school safety team will use a subcommittee to create their anti-bullying plan. The subcommittee should be no larger than five to six members who represent a cross-section of individuals from the community, school faculty, parents, law enforcement, and juvenile justice. A student from the school safety team should also be a member of the subcommittee. As with school safety and crisis response planning teams, anti-bullying committee members should be cross-functional and represent a diversity of backgrounds in order to obtain the most complete plan (Seeger, Barton, Heyart, & Bultnyck, 2001).

Traditionally, school safety teams play an active role in the development of a school safety plan, and often assist with its implementation, reviewing and modifying the plan according to the school's needs. Members from different backgrounds will usually produce more comprehensive school safety plans that best address the needs of the school and the ways in which to facilitate the plan. Most school safety teams will include a representative from the juvenile justice system, such as a judge, law enforcement official, or prosecuting attorney; a mental health specialist, such as a psychologist, counselor, or social worker; a government official, such as a mayor or city council member; a community representative, such as a person providing afterschool programming; and a parent, teacher, and student. Although many schools develop school safety teams on a building-by-building basis, it is more beneficial to establish school safety plans and teams on a district level.

It is important that the school safety team members remain on the team for at least 2 years, so that the team will have some consistency. Once the committee becomes established, however, term limits and graduated schedules of member rotations should be enacted. In this case, new members will bring new ideas and new energy to the issue of school safety.

If the school safety plan is districtwide and the anti-bullying initiative is on a school-by-school basis, try to develop a subcommittee using representatives from the larger school safety team, yet adding appropriate school faculty, parents, and youth from the school. Students are key in developing a successful schoolwide anti-bullying campaign. Students need to be involved in developing anti-bullying policies and giving input on the disciplinary measures taken to deal with bullying behaviors. Their input is invaluable when determining the types of programming necessary for the school and its constituents.

ANTI-BULLYING WITHIN THE CONTEXT OF THE SAFE SCHOOL PLAN

Integrating the anti-bullying program within the safe school plan is a valuable exercise for schools. Anti-bullying initiatives should not be considered separate from the school safety plan; they are a specific extension of most youth violence prevention and crisis management programming.

In most cases, anti-bullying initiatives may be cleanly placed within the current school safety plan. As outlined by Barton in *Leadership Strategies for Safe Schools* (2000), school safety plans should address a variety of issues, including:

- Environmental safety
- Student education
- School-community partnerships

- Policies and procedures
- Mission statement

The case study of Flavell Middle School is used to illustrate the connection of school safety plan components and typical anti-bullying efforts.

CASE STUDY: FLAVELL MIDDLE SCHOOL

Flavell Middle School is located in a suburb of a large metropolitan city. The school district has recently readjusted the school boundaries, such that the once predominately upper-middle-class school now serves upper-lower-class students living on the northeast and southwest borders of the community. Due to the boundary expansion, student enrollment has increased in one year from a population of 600 to more than 1,250 students. The school is now racially diverse, with 30 percent Asian American, 20 percent Hispanic American, 10 percent European American, 15 percent African American, and 25 percent Arab American. Approximately 50 percent of all students use the private school bus transportation, and 65 percent qualify for the free lunch program. Since the redistricting, standardized test scores have declined more than 30 percent.

School administration consists of an Asian American male principal, an Arab American female assistant principal, and an African American female assistant principal. The school employs 33 teachers (45 percent European American, 25 percent African American, and 30 percent Hispanic American), two counselors (50 percent European and 50 percent African American) and six support staff members (100 percent Hispanic American).

School staff has demonstrated a decrease in tolerance for working with each other on special school programs. Staff meetings erupt on a regular basis and frequently end with several teachers being verbally abusive (for example, engaging in name calling) toward the school principal. Teaching staff complain that counselors are not available to children needing support. Counselors are supervising the in-school suspension room, referred to as the "JD" (juvenile delinquent) room, an average of 20 hours a week for 60–75 students.

In the past year, school administrators have handled increased numbers of criminal acts on the school buses. Students have committed assaults (sexual and physical) and robberies, and regularly engage in verbal bullying while waiting for the school buses. Bus drivers have made formal complaints to both the school administration and their union.

Student conflicts and acts of violence have increased greatly during lunchtime. Due to increased student population and inadequate lunchroom facilities, students who qualify for free lunch programs are required to remain in the hallway until other students have been seated for lunch. Physical, verbal, and relational bullying is rampant during this period of time.

Classroom conflicts have increased during the past year. Students often complain about working with "other" students in cooperative activities. Significant peer group polarization is occurring in the hallway. Increasingly, culturally insensitive graffiti has been placed upon bathroom walls, in hallways, on buses, and on exterior school walls.

The parent-teacher organization (PTO) is almost nonfunctional. The leadership does not embrace or support new members from the northeast and southwest area.

Environmental Safety

School safety plans should include information on maintaining environmental safety through policies and procedures for controlling access to the school building and security practices for the building. Environmental safety concerns in a school safety plan are critical and relevant to anti-bullying programming because bullying behavior may occur in specific, low-traffic, dark areas of the schools. Schools may wish to develop safe areas in their school safety plan where victimized students can go following a bullying episode. These locations must be closely supervised with the understanding that the areas are to provide short-term refuge rather than long-term solutions. Following a survey of students (see Figure 3.2 for a sample form), identify the locations and times in which students feel most vulnerable or unsafe. Use this information to review or develop the school safety plan specific to environmental concerns. Think about developing ways to provide adequate supervision in places and at times that students identify. Reactive approaches to school safety, such as surveillance equipment to capture physical bullying episodes, may also be identified in the anti-bullying plan.

The anti-bullying plan should also include a careful analysis of the playground area—the most common site of bullying, particularly in elementary grades. Environmental factors such as unstructured play areas may foster bullying and exclusion and increase boredom, competition, and conflict if resources are scarce. Playground areas should encourage activities suitable to all children, with areas available for running games such as football and solitary play areas such as an imaginary game area or working garden. Playground changes need not be expensive, as costs may be offset by community partners (assisting with the costs of landscaping) and projects may be maintained through parent involvement (encouraging parents to help with the working garden).

In the case of Flavell Middle School, it is clear that several environmental considerations are important for anti-bullying efforts. First, the lunchroom structure, in which students who receive free lunch are differentiated from those who do not, is getting in the way of a safe environment and increasing the likelihood for bullying behaviors to occur. The anti-bullying plan must address this environmental issue by eliminating the differentiation of students at lunch. A second environmental issue is occurring on and around the buses. The anti-bullying plan may address this environmental concern by providing supervisors on buses or staggering the departure times of grades. Finally, the culturally insensitive graffiti on school grounds has the potential to be aggressive toward one or more students, increasing the likelihood for bullying behaviors. If the graffiti is confined to a specific place in the school, additional personnel may patrol the area, or it may be treated to prevent spray paint and other destructive materials.

Student Education

Education programming for students is also a critical component of school safety plans that may be extended to include anti-bullying programming. Team members may wish to consider a number of key questions regarding how the school will implement student education programming concerning anti-bullying. Will curriculum be purchased for students, or will programming be infused throughout a particular course? If the school safety plan already calls for a peer mediation program, will it be expanded to include an anti-bullying component? Also, the subcommittee should address the need for professional development on the issue. How does the programming fit with the culture of the school, and is it appropriate for the student population?

The case of Flavell Middle School indicates the need for student education. In this case, students are demonstrating increased conflict, intolerance toward others (race and socioeconomically based), and bullying behaviors. In addition, the high numbers of students engaged in the in-school suspension room may indicate that a student education program is necessary. To best address Flavell's issues, student education is important. School administrators and staff may best infuse anti-bullying curriculum through classroom work, particularly with the use of cooperative learning interactions. In this case, anti-bullying efforts should also bridge the school's diversity issues (race, socioeconomics).

School-Community Partnerships

School safety plans should also consider building and maintaining school-community partnerships. Anti-bullying subcommittees may find these relationships particularly helpful. Some schools use community business partners to provide incentives for students to intervene in bullying situations. The Safe Streets program in Detroit, Michigan, offered by the NCCJ (National Conference for Community and Justice)-Michigan Region and the Youth Connection, created a network of business supporters along routes to and from schools. These partners often assist in intervening when witnessing bullying situations among children walking to and from school, in addition to providing safe havens for youth seeking refuge from unsafe situations. In other cases, parents or guardians help to support schools by serving as noon aides and bus stop supervisors. These types of school-community partnerships may increase the supervision of potentially "hot" locations in the school, thus reducing bullying behaviors.

In the case of Flavell Middle School, the partnerships between administrators and parents or guardians are integral for decreasing bullying among the students in the school. The intolerance demonstrated by the seasoned students toward the newly enrolled students may be a reflection of the parents' or guardians' intolerance toward the newcomers. Providing support and education for the PTO group may help facilitate more constructive relations between students and parents or guardians.

Policies and Procedures

School safety plans must also include the potential for revising or developing school policies and procedures. Districtwide policies and procedures regarding anti-bullying must be included and applied to school-based safety planning. For schools without supporting districtwide policies and procedures, development is a necessary first step toward building an anti-bullying campaign that succeeds. Indeed, one policy that may need to be developed is one addressing the confidential reporting system that allows children to report victimization and that records the details of the bullying incidents.

Once anti-bullying campaign committee members have reviewed or created the school safety plans and considered the implications within the district plan, the committee is ready to develop a more complete schoolwide anti-bullying plan.

Flavell Middle School is in desperate need of revised policies and procedures that will impact the organization now and in the future. First, staff meetings must be conducted in a constructive way. Consequences, including formal reprimands, are necessary for the school administration to gain some control over the situation. Next, the in-school suspension must be reviewed for changes in policies and procedures, as it is being used too frequently and is being supervised with highly skilled persons. Student-staff ratios also must be reviewed, as the increased student enrollment has substantially increased the demands on the current staff.

Mission Statement

In addition, the anti-bullying committee may wish to develop a mission statement that supports the proposed policies and procedures. This mission statement should include a goal for the school and the anti-bullying committee and an explanation of how the goal can be achieved, from the perspective of all members of the school community.

ELEMENTS OF A SCHOOLWIDE ANTI-BULLYING PLAN

Figure 3.3 identifies the elements of a schoolwide anti-bullying plan. Policies and procedures, staff development, student education, schoolwide programming, and family and parent involvement are discussed in this section of the chapter, while monitoring and evaluation are discussed in Chapter 6.

Creating and Reviewing Policies and Procedures

The purpose of an anti-bullying policy is to promote a consistent approach and to create a climate in which all types of bullying are regarded as unacceptable. The anti-bullying policies should have very clear goals and objectives that are necessary to develop appropriate programming. Anti-bullying policies usually share a common goal: to promote a safe and secure learning environment for students, free from threat, harassment, and bullying (physical, verbal, relational, sexual). The anti-bullying policy is an important step in creating a safe school climate that allows victims or witnesses to bullying to relax and focus their attention on learning rather than staying safe. School policymaking need not be complex. See Figure 3.4 for issues to consider and steps to take when creating a school policy on bullying.

Figure 3.3   Elements of a Schoolwide Anti-Bullying Plan

- Policies and procedures
- Staff development
- Student education programming
- Parent involvement
- Monitoring and evaluation

Figure 3.4   Developing a School Policy on Bullying

1. Understand the state legislation (if any) and local school district's policy before proposing school policies. Be sure to be consistent with state and local initiatives. Chapter 7 provides some guidance on legislative trends in anti-bullying.

2. Define bullying behaviors in your school. Most will include physical, verbal, relational, and sexual aggression and/or the perceived threat.

3. What are your goals for the anti-bullying policy in your school?
   - Is your policy aimed at preventing bullying and victimization behaviors? Or, is your policy designed to be reactive to bullying behavior in the school?
   - Will the policy cover management of bullying behavior while it occurs in the school?
   - Will the bullying policy add to your current policies of school discipline or school safety, or will it be separate?
   - Will the school policy also include bullying as part of a broad social skills training educational program? Is it part of a larger school safety plan, or is it separate?

4. Determine what the policy will look like.
   - What types of elements will be included: Will it outline how anti-bullying will be dealt with through the curriculum?
   - Will it outline supervision of key areas in the school (cover only certain areas)?
   - Will it provide information on how investigations of bullying will occur?
   - Will it offer guidelines for punishment of policy violations, such as suspension or expulsion?
   - Will it provide alternative education guidelines for listening to victims, witnesses, and bullies?
   - How will notification of the parents work? As a team, develop the types of disciplinary action that should be taken against bullies, depending on circumstances.

5. Identify procedures for communicating bullying behaviors to parents.

6. Develop a process of communicating disciplinary actions on a classroom basis.

7. Decide responsibilities and roles. Who intends to do what, and when, to develop and implement the policy? Will the principal handle the punitive part? Will counselors handle the hearing/listening part?

8. How will the policy be disseminated?

Staffing During Lunch and Recess

Unsupervised times during the school day, particularly on the playground, are the most likely times for bullying behavior among children. When reviewing school policies and procedures, creating a plan for controlling the playground setting is an important step in building an anti-bullying campaign in your school. One way to improve supervision while students are on the playground is to increase the number of adults available. Although there is consensus that increasing the number of supervisors on the playground will decrease the likelihood of bullying behaviors (particularly physical behaviors), in most cases, it is not an economical solution. In addition, use of teachers during these times on a voluntary basis is not guaranteed to improve the number of adults because school faculty use lunchtime for a variety of other important activities.

Schools may be able to increase the number of adults by recruiting volunteers. In addition, schools that receive federal Safe and Drug-Free funds or community funding often use some of these monies to pay additional lunchtime supervisors for security reasons.

An alternative to increasing the number of adults is to hone the skills of current lunchtime supervisors, making them more aware of bullying behaviors and more prepared to intervene and prevent such situations. When developing polices and procedures for the anti-bullying campaign, consider providing further training for individuals currently working (Mellor, 1991). Until recently, lunchroom supervisors and playground attendants (traditionally parents or community residents) have served as untapped resources in the battle for improving school safety. Consider providing development for playground supervisors that includes:

- Identifying bullying behavior (which differs from rough and tumble play)
- Intervening in bullying situations
- Building positive student-supervisor relationships, and
- Encouraging socially appropriate and cooperative interaction on the playground

Designing and Implementing Staff Development

Staff development is an important component of schoolwide anti-bullying initiatives. If the anti-bullying committee decides to implement schoolwide programming, such as peer mediation or a specific anti-bullying curriculum, school faculty must be highly prepared to support the programming initiatives and implement curriculum components of the initiative. Before anti-bullying initiatives begin, staff orientation and professional development opportunities must occur.

The best approach to preparing and enlisting staff support for programming initiatives in the school is to provide separate sessions for program orientations and staff development. Staff should be provided with extensive information concerning the anti-bullying initiatives, how staff will be involved, what policies and procedures will occur and when, and how individuals may volunteer to assist with the initiative. It is important to also include a brief overview of the issue of bullying and how social skills training programs benefit academic competency in children while at the same time building safer school communities.

Staff development training should occur prior to implementation of the anti-bullying initiatives. (See Figure 3.5 for sample training ideas.) Staff should review results of the student assessment and staff assessment

Figure 3.5   Inservice Training Ideas

Agenda 1

A. Recognizing a bully-victim relationship
B. Understanding possible causes and correlates of bullying and victimization behaviors
C. Assessing bully-victim relationships
D. Analyzing effects of bullying behavior (short- and long-term)
E. Understanding school and state policies regarding bullying behaviors

Agenda 2

A. Intervention strategies for bullying behaviors in the classroom
B. Prevention and anti-bullying programs for the classroom
C. Integration of conflict resolution strategies into the curriculum for anti-bullying effects

---

(if conducted) of bullying in the school and the definitions of bully-victim relationships. Short- and long-term consequences of bullying behavior also should be discussed.

Additional staff development will be required if the school has selected a specific anti-bullying curriculum that must be taught in the classroom. Anti-bullying committee members may also wish to include anti-bullying intervention and prevention techniques to the meeting agenda. If schools have not already conducted professional development trainings for violence prevention or conflict resolution education, then anti-bullying training may be folded into these important topics.

Staff development is one of the best methods for improving support for anti-bullying initiatives. Once staff members are familiar with the program and its benefits, they often volunteer to implement additional components of the anti-bullying campaign. Although staff members might not be directly involved in programming, particularly if no schoolwide curriculum is being used, the relationship between staff knowledge and support and program effectiveness and stability is quite high.

Implementing Student Education Programming

Schools face challenges to implementing schoolwide anti-bullying programming that go beyond the regulation of policies and procedures within the school building. Schoolwide initiatives may involve the use of anti-bullying curriculum, discussed in the next chapter. Schoolwide curriculum is often implemented unsuccessfully in a nonstandardized fashion and used in isolation, making curriculum the only mechanism used to battle bullying. Schoolwide curriculum implementation depends upon the support of all faculty, some of whom may not agree that the time expended for such programming is worthwhile. Therefore, curriculum should be supplemented by schoolwide programming initiatives that involve the whole school, using various types of programs and methods of implementation.

The schoolwide initiatives outlined next can have a substantial impact on the school climate, with very little effort expended by school faculty. Ideally, election of a schoolwide curriculum and implementation of additional programming measures will promote the greatest changes in bullying behaviors in the school.

Bully Courts

Bully courts are implemented in some schools as a means of reducing bullying behavior. A cadre of students is extensively trained to serve as arbitrators or judges who preside over the bully court. Following a bully-victim incident, students or adults may request the process through an anonymous referral system. Unlike mediation, bully courts are implemented in most schools on a mandatory basis to defer or replace in-school suspensions and detentions. Bullies and their victims, along with witnesses, are asked to explain the circumstances of the situation to a panel of bully court representatives. These representatives are then asked to judge their peers and devise appropriate punishment for the behaviors. Adult mentorship and administration are extremely important, because the court system, not the disputants, determines the outcome of the court hearing. European schools frequently use bully courts, but they are highly controversial in the United States because children determine the consequences for their peers. Several schools in New Jersey use bully courts and cite that they are very effective.

Peer Counseling

Peer counseling (peer support) is another schoolwide strategy that has been used to prevent and intervene in cases of bullying. Usually used in secondary schools, peer counseling involves training a group of students who assist and support victims of bullying. Peer counselors are not intended to be used for purposes of therapy, but rather as a mechanism for students who have been bullied to talk and to know that a social support network is available. Peer counselors are also useful for disseminating information on options for the victim, such as the mediation process. Often, peer counselors are scheduled throughout the day and may be placed in one of the safe rooms described later in this chapter. Cowie (1998) found that peer counseling resulted in immediate and long-term effects that were beneficial to vulnerable students; it improved the school climate and enhanced the personal qualities of the peer counselors themselves.

Bully Boxes

Schools often require confidential and/or anonymous methods of reporting bullying behavior. Bully boxes may be used as a technique for students to write their concerns and place the information in a locked box that guarantees confidentiality. (A sample bullying reporting form is shown in Figure 3.6.) Boxes should be locked and placed in at least three locations schoolwide: next to the cafeteria, next to the main office, and near the mediation or safe room. A program administrator should collect the anti-bullying reporting forms at least twice each day and determine if the situations should be handled further through peer counseling or bully courts (if the school provides these programs). In order for the bully boxes to assist in anti-bullying school initiatives, reporting forms must remain confidential, and the administration should not use them to discipline students. Rather, the purpose of the reporting forms is to provide a mechanism for use of the available programming initiatives. Reporting forms are also a convenient way for administrators to maintain records of patterns of behavior.

School Safety Hotlines

Recently, schools have selected telephone hotlines as an anonymous way for students to identify threats of potential violence, bullying behaviors, and substance abuse or criminal activity of other students. Schools should use hotlines differently from bullying boxes or referral boxes, especially if the school administration plans to use the information for punitive purposes. Often, law enforcement agencies supervise hotlines and monitor them for criminal acts. Occasionally law enforcement connects the hotlines to 911 emergency lines to provide the ability to quickly respond to potential threats. In other cases, hotlines are implemented within the school building and are used to provide anonymous tips regarding potential gang activity or violence, or to report bullying behaviors.

Telephone hotlines may also be used to provide support to students afraid to speak out about bullying. The fact, however, that students select the hotlines is a signal that some schools may not be providing opportunities for students to discuss problems openly. Telephone hotlines may also introduce liability for the school if a student calls the hotline seeking assistance and the result is violence against the student or school. Therefore, internal telephone hotlines may not be the best route for schools. Often, it is helpful to collaborate with local mental health agencies that already have telephone hotlines so that the help hotlines are publicized widely within the school, and agency personnel are prepared for calls that might involve bullying behaviors. Working closely with a mental health agency will also alleviate some of the liability, maintain the confidentiality of the caller, and provide the best, most trained personnel to assist students who need help.

It is extremely important for administrators to use the hotlines differently than the referral boxes and to be sure that students understand the important differences. Hotlines are more frequently used for disciplinary or punitive actions than are referral boxes, which are used more for

Figure 3.6   Sample Anti-Bullying Reporting Form

Date: _____

Names of the student(s) involved in the bullying incident:

_____

Where did the incident occur?   What did the incident involve?

_____ Classroom   _____ Name calling

_____ Hallway   _____ Pushing/Shoving

_____ Cafeteria   _____ Teasing

_____ Outside   _____ Other

_____ Other

When did this occur? _____

Briefly describe the bullying incident:

_____

_____

_____

_____

_____

Suggested method for handling the incident:

_____Bully court_____Peer counseling_____Other

Person requesting support:

_____Student_____Teacher_____Counselor_____Administrator___Other

Name of person requesting mediation (optional):

_____

reconciliation or resolution between two or more parties. Hotlines have become quite controversial due to their anonymous nature and the potential consequences to individuals identified as a "threat." For instance, a school in a suburb of Detroit, Michigan, decided to install the hotline for school safety. Students quickly learned that they could call in "enemies" to get them in trouble because just giving a name and an anticipated action would cause the school administrators to take disciplinary action. In contrast, bully boxes and mediation boxes can be quite effective and require more information (although confidential), which is then screened for accuracy before the school takes nondisciplinary action.

Several states, including Indiana and Kansas, have initiated school violence hotlines as a measure of reporting. State departments of education have teamed up with law enforcement, principally state police departments (as in Michigan), to institute anonymous telephone hotlines. Calls are directed to 1-800 numbers and are then transferred to local emergency monitoring systems (911). Hotlines are relatively new, and their effectiveness in curbing youth violence in schools has yet to be carefully evaluated.

Safe Rooms

Some schools have created safe rooms to serve as a refuge for bullied students. These rooms are often empty classrooms supervised by support personnel. These rooms may be open during breaks and lunchtimes. Often, schools will use the mediation room as the safe room. Safe rooms may be very important for victims; however, these rooms will only provide safety in the short term and do not teach victims assertiveness or other skills to help reduce the likelihood that the bullying will occur again. Safe rooms should not be used as a sole programming method, but rather as a temporary mechanism for victims as the school transitions to an anti-bullying school environment. Continuing safe rooms beyond the transition period might suggest to victims that the rest of the school is more hostile than it truly is.

Involving Family Members

Whole school anti-bullying initiatives should incorporate students' parents and guardians as much as possible to

- Ensure their support for programming
- Build rapport and recruit volunteers among parents and guardians for anti-bullying programming
- Educate parents and guardians on bullying behaviors and parenting practices and their relationship to bully-victim-witness relationships, and
- Support staffing needs and fill gaps during highly volatile lunchroom and playground times

Family members of students may become involved in the anti-bullying initiatives in a number of ways, including:

- Participating in the anti-bullying plan committee
- Attending orientation and educational development meetings at the school, and
- Volunteering to publicize the initiatives or raise funds for programming

In addition, parents play a pivotal role in assisting in anti-bullying initiatives by identifying bully-victim-witness behaviors in their own children, teaching their children more appropriate interpersonal skills and methods for using the skills, and serving as models who express themselves constructively in interpersonal relationships.

Anti-bullying committee members should be prepared to support and educate parents about bullying. They should create short, direct-mail literature inviting parents to review the extensive resources at the school. Parents should be advised of the elements of the whole school plan for anti-bullying and given helpful hints to use in the home. A sample of important information to share with parents and guardians is provided in Figure 3.7.

SUMMARY

Developing an effective anti-bullying program is a complex task that demands the involvement of students, parents, teachers, administrators,

Figure 3.7   Checklist for Parent Information Sheet

In letter or educational materials for parents and guardians:
1. Identify components of the anti-bullying initiatives including changes in policies/procedures regarding suspension, detention, and expulsions for bullying behaviors.

2. Provide statistics of bullying behavior in the school (as provided by the student survey).

3. List ways that parents may become involved in the anti-bullying initiatives, including the time commitment or level of training necessary to volunteer.

4. Encourage parents and guardians to talk to their children about how they are being treated by other peers as a mechanism to diagnose potential bullying.

5. Alert parents on what to look for, such as a significant change in behavioral, sleeping, eating, or play patterns; torn clothes; grade changes; or needing extra money.

6. Provide methods for parents and guardians to tell school administrators if they suspect bullying-victim behavior in their children.

7. Outline ways that parents and guardians may educate their children on bullying-victim relationships, including methods of rewarding kindness and tolerance toward others when intervening in a bullying episode.

and the community at large. Whether the plan develops on a classroom level or districtwide, it takes time to create and implement. Student surveys designed to measure the scope of the existing problem are a common starting place. From there, programming can be designed to raise student and staff awareness of what constitutes bullying and how it can be managed. Everyone involved needs to be trained to recognize his or her role: from parents who can learn how to spot and minimize their child's bullying or victimization to students themselves who may help solve the problem through their participation in peer counseling or bully courts. The most successful anti-bullying programs are those that approach the problem systematically and involve everyone in the solution.

4

Strategies for Managing and Preventing Bullying Behavior in the Classroom

The whole school approach to anti-bullying is preferable to the classroom approach, as it provides the best foundation for changing all schoolchildren's knowledge, skills, and attitudes regarding bullying behaviors. However, much work in the prevention and management of bully-victim relationships may be accomplished at the classroom level.

The effectiveness of classroom management and prevention strategies in curbing bullying behaviors, however, depends largely on classroom teachers' perceptions and attitudes toward bully-victim relationships. Research conducted in Europe and Scandinavia supports the impact of teachers' perceptions of bullying behavior and the likelihood of those teachers to prevent, manage, or intervene during bullying episodes in the classroom.

Until recently, teachers may not have felt comfortable intervening in bully-victim relationships because of a false belief that an intervention might create more serious problems for the victim in the future. Jeffrey, Miller, and Linn (2001) stated that a general attitude among teachers and school administrators continues to be that interpersonal aggression, or meanness, is a normative developmental feature of middle school students. Only recently have researchers discounted bullying as a harmful rite of passage for children, now recognizing the serious consequences that may result from such relationships. School faculty has responded quickly to the latest research by developing their own skills and learning how to teach children to handle bully-victim-witness relationships. However, too often school staff may be unaware of what bullying behaviors look like or may not know how to manage the behaviors or prevent them from occurring. Researchers have identified that teachers intervene in bullying episodes only in a minority of cases, perhaps because they are not aware that the episodes are occurring (Atlas & Pepler, 1998; Craig & Pepler, 1997). Other teachers believe that social skills training programs need not be taught in school, and that the teacher's sole responsibility is academic competency.

Often, teachers are unprepared for handling bullying behaviors. Many education schools across the country do not cover social skill development and school safety as core courses; bullying behaviors are often not addressed unless the issue is covered during a discussion of classroom management strategies. Given the current literature on school bullying and its potential relationship to school violence, teaching professionals' attitudes toward their responsibilities in teaching, intervening, and preventing destructive conflict resolution strategies have begun to change. Almost as important, teachers must consider children's social skill development, because research shows that more socially sophisticated children are also children who excel academically. Providing bullied children with opportunities to build their self-esteem, self-competence, and future academic success is the responsibility of all teachers in K–12 classrooms.

MANAGEMENT VERSUS PREVENTION TECHNIQUES

Often, issues of classroom management become intertwined with prevention programming, particularly when dealing with social skill development. Teachers need classroom management techniques to deal with disruptive students who interfere with the learning process of their peers. Classroom management techniques might be useful to handle students who challenge the teacher and other students, who are disrespectful, refuse to adhere to classroom rules, and do not comply when asked to participate. In these examples, classroom management clearly is necessary for the classroom environment to be renewed to one of learning. Prevention techniques often overlap classroom management techniques; however, they should be used in the classroom setting for different purposes. Prevention techniques are useful when they are intended to prevent the expression of behaviors that interfere with classroom management. For instance, developing constructive social relationships in the classroom may reduce the

Figure 4.1   Classroom Management Strategies

Preparedness: Teachers with effective classrooms have developed a number of methods for handling student issues, similar to a series of file drawers. The file drawers contain diverse options, including environmental or structural resolutions to issues of classroom management as well as a variety of potential responses to appropriate or inappropriate behaviors.

Responsiveness: To create effective learning environments, teachers also must be responsive to classroom management issues. Ignoring inappropriate behaviors informs students that their behavior does not have consequences and is therefore validated and can be duplicated. Teachers with effective management styles also respond unemotionally to classroom situations. Although it is difficult to do, maintaining composure during a volatile classroom challenge makes teachers better able to de-escalate and effectively manage situations than they would be if they were to respond with heightened levels of emotion.

Consistency: Not only should teachers be prepared to respond to classroom management challenges immediately, but they also should be consistent in responding to inappropriate behaviors in the classroom.

---

need for classroom management when using cooperative or group activities. In contrast, classroom management techniques do not necessarily teach children the skills needed to prevent future behaviors.

Eliminating bullying behaviors often requires school faculty members to use both classroom management techniques and prevention techniques. Bullying behaviors often occur in the classroom setting and may occur during cooperative or group activities or even during structured instruction time.

Classroom management resources often focus on a number of strategies that are most useful in handling classroom situations including bullying episodes. See Figure 4.1 for categories of classroom management strategies.

These classroom management techniques may be applied to anti-bullying management in the classroom as outlined in Figure 4.2.

PREVENTION STRATEGIES

Prevention of bullying-victim behaviors in the classroom is important for building an effective learning and socially inclusive environment. To implement prevention strategies, teachers must be prepared to spend some time during class to work with students, using unconventional teaching methods covering untraditional topics. For instance, teachers must be comfortable providing students with classroom time to dialogue with each other about personal experiences involving social interactions. Instruction time in core areas is often reduced to accommodate the need to build classroom settings that are safe and free from bullying behaviors, yet in the long term classroom settings are more conclusive to learning.

Figure 4.2   Classroom Management Techniques for Bullying Behavior

---

Preparedness

- Prepare a list of techniques that you may use to defuse situations in the classroom setting.
- Learn to identify bullying behaviors in the classroom and understand how classroom structure, cooperative learning group composition, and social skills training programs may prevent the need for management strategies.

Responsiveness

- Respond firmly to reports of bullying in the classroom. Avoid an overly punitive response to bullies, as it models authoritarian methods of resolving conflict.
- Never ignore the bullying behaviors by redirecting the group unless using this technique to address the bullying behavior in private. Ignoring the bullying behavior reinforces its expression in the classroom and the teacher's acceptance of it.
- Confront the bully with the victim present, either after class or when the incident can be addressed without heightened emotion. Never confront the bully in front of the classroom, as it provides a larger audience in front of which a bully may continue the taunting.

Consistency

- Decisive responses must occur every time when bullying behavior is observed or reported by students in the classroom.

A number of strategies are useful in preventing bully-victim relationships in the classroom setting. Before teachers embark on implementing a bully-free environment in the classroom, they should assess student perceptions of bullying behaviors. (See Chapter 3, Figure 3.2, for a sample assessment survey instrument.) Besides assessing individual perceptions of bullying behaviors, teachers may ask students to use a measure of peer popularity (for example, sociometric nomination) as a tool to assist the teacher with identifying students who may be at risk for bullying/victimization (see Figure 4.3). Doll, Siemers, Nickolite, and Song (2003) demonstrated how teachers and a consultant examined a classroom environment using the ClassMap procedure and facilitated discussions among middle school students as a means of preventing classroom bullying. To understand student dynamics in a broad sense, teachers may provide students with the following task:

Ask each student to respond to each of the following items:

- Name two students you would invite to your birthday party.
- Name two students whom you would not invite to your birthday party.
- Name two students who get picked on by others.
- Name two students who pick on other students.

Figure 4.3   Peer Network Sociogram for the Classroom

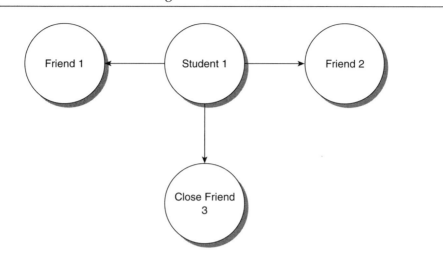

Data may be summarized by number of student responses or through the development of a classroom's social network. For instance, teachers may be interested in identifying students with strong peer relations. Teachers may count the number of "birthday invitations" a student would receive as a measure of peer popularity and thus, social support. Students with the least number of invitations, therefore, could be at risk for victimization by bullies. Respondents would remain anonymous through this technique. Teachers also may ask students to place their names on responses as a means of creating a peer network sociogram for the classroom. Through this technique, teachers can create a map of friendships, producing information on students who are excluded and at risk for victimization.

These exercises will assist teachers in further understanding students' perceptions regarding others in the class. The exercise may also assist teachers and school leaders with more careful observation of the classroom as a means of preventing bullying behavior.

Once teachers have identified perceptions of bullying behaviors, understand student needs, and have created a social map of the class, they may implement specific strategies or programming.

Teacher-Student Relationships

The greatest mechanism for preventing bullying and victimization in the classroom is to develop the quality of the teacher-student relationship with all students in the classroom. Building rapport with students in the classroom has several important outcomes, which tend to influence any anti-bullying classroom initiatives. As well, supervision and discipline of student behavior will contribute greatly to building more constructive teacher-student relationships.

First, developing the quality of the teacher's relationship with all students will enable victims to feel comfortable sharing their experiences. Too often, students feel uncomfortable disclosing bullying episodes to teaching faculty because they are unsure of how the teacher will react. Discomfort with the teaching relationship is the most common reason for students to hide bullying behaviors.

Next, quality student-teacher relationships will improve the likelihood of students disclosing bullying behaviors occurring in the classroom. Similarly, witnesses to bullying behaviors will be supported to intervene if they possess a better relationship with the classroom teacher.

Finally, social skills training programs are more effective when teachers have strong interpersonal relationships with students. In the case of social skill prevention programs, the messenger must be able to model constructive interpersonal strategies with students in order to effect individual changes.

To reinforce prosocial behaviors that occur between students and within the teacher-student relationship, teachers should consistently acknowledge and reward them. Conversely, careful supervision and discipline of negative behaviors are critical not only for classroom management but also as a prevention strategy against bullying behaviors in the classroom. Teachers need to educate themselves on definitions of bullying, identification of bullying behaviors in the classroom, and methods for assessing and observing bully-victim relationships in the classroom. This knowledge will assist teachers in appropriately supervising the classroom setting, particularly with knowing what types of bullying and victimization behaviors will occur in the classroom and what they look like. Developing a repertoire of possible methods for dealing with classroom management issues is an important step for supervising the classroom and preventing bullying behaviors.

Methods for disciplining students may also be used to prevent bully-victim relationships from flourishing in the classroom. The responsibility of classroom discipline may be shared among students and the teacher when handling student-student conflict situations.

A common prevention strategy for teachers is to provide an opportunity for students to assist in developing consequences for inappropriate behaviors in the classroom. Students should identify the types of offenses they perceive as bullying behaviors and resulting disciplinary actions. Some teachers will also develop consequences for bullying supporters and witnesses who do not intervene in bullying episodes. In cases where bullying occurs, teachers are supported for disciplining the students because the consequences have been developed by the classroom, hence shifting responsibility from the teacher's wishes to the wishes of all classroom participants. When developing disciplinary guidelines in the classroom, however, be sure that these guidelines are in compliance with any school or district measures involving bullying behaviors. Behaviors and resulting consequences should be prominently posted in the classroom.

In a related fashion, teachers and students may create a class code of conduct to supplement the disciplinary guidelines they have developed (see Figure 4.4). Teachers should consider implementing several lessons on awareness of bullying and prosocial behaviors prior to developing the code. Literature is an excellent starting point. Consider using the Berenstain Bears (Berenstain & Berenstain, *The Berenstain Bears and Too Much Teasing*, 1995) for elementary school children and *Lord of the Flies* by William Golding (1954) with older students. While discussing the books, teachers may lead a discussion on bullying, identifying bullying behaviors and how bullying feels and affects people. Students may then generate a list of prosocial behaviors to combat bullying as the basis for the classroom code of conduct.

Environment

Teachers play a critical role in developing a safe and inclusive classroom for all students. This is particularly important when preventing and intervening in bullying situations. Regardless of the type of curriculum they use (direct instruction with an anti-bullying curriculum or direct infusion of concepts), teachers should begin to develop a respectful, civilized classroom as early in the semester as possible. Espelage and Asidao (2001) recommend that secondary teachers may address relational bullying behaviors by promoting the respect of individual differences among students. Early adolescents' social worlds center around small, intimate peer groups that are often formed on the bases of shared interests and activities (Ennett & Bauman, 1996). As such, students are more likely to seek similarities and affiliation with peers. As peer groups become more distinctive, bullying behaviors increase within the context of an us-versus-them mentality. Given the developmental context, teachers should promote genuine respect of individual differences as a means of preventing bullying behavior in the classroom.

Dialogue is one technique useful for building inclusive middle school classroom settings. Dialogue is a purposeful discussion. The goal of dialogue

Figure 4.4   Our No-Bullying Classroom Rules

- We won't bully other students.
- We will stop bullies by speaking up and by helping other students who are being bullied.
- We will tell adults when we see or hear about bullying and ask for help.
- We will learn how to resolve conflict in peaceful ways.

is to search for understanding rather than agreements or solutions. Dialogue requires the teacher to become a facilitator for participation and a guide for self-discovery rather than a leader and educator imparting knowledge to others. If the school has created a whole school approach to anti-bullying, often teams of teachers will spend one planning period every 2 weeks, rotating in other classrooms to allow for impartiality, to serve as facilitators of dialogue sessions. Sometimes dialogue is difficult for teachers because it requires them to take a different role with the students, empowering students to learn through each other in a nontraditional fashion. Dialogue is a highly effective tool, particularly in the middle and high school grades, because it enables individuals to reflect on their own experiences (introspection) before thinking about how these experiences may affect their behavior toward others. See Figure 4.5 for some dialogue guidelines.

Dialogue may also be used in conjunction with curriculum implementation, providing students with an opportunity to use the skills that they are learning through direct instruction of the other curriculum. Students will be able to use techniques important for developing skills such as

Figure 4.5   Dialogue Guidelines

1. Describe the purpose of dialogue to students. A good dialogue will include the opportunity to:
   - Listen to and be listened to such that all youth will be heard
   - Develop or deepen mutual understanding of each other
   - Speak and be spoken to in a respectful manner
   - Learn about the perspective of others and reflect on one's own views

This will assist students in identifying rules (step 2) that will help the group build trust.

2. Identify rules for dialogue that are separate from the classroom rules. Tell students that you intend to use classroom dialogue often and need everyone to feel comfortable sharing opinions, ideas, and beliefs. Make sure you clearly shift into the dialogue mode by pointing to the rules when the session begins and when it ends. (Have students generate the rules on their own. Post them in visible spots in the classroom. Amend them on a regular basis. Do not add any rules on which the group does not agree. The only rule that is very important is the confidentiality rule.)

3. Design the classroom for dialogue; have desks or chairs placed in a circle (if possible) to allow students to see everyone. Have the group practice with dialogue by starting with examples such as "My favorite television show is . . . ," or "The worst thing that has ever happened to me was . . . ," or "The best thing is . . . ," and move toward thinking about what friendship means. Teachers should be part of the circle and not separated from it, yet should not be participants in the dialogue.

4. One of the main goals of the dialogue group is to encourage all participants to feel safe to share their own experience and opinions. However, students should not be called upon to respond in the group unless they wish to do so. Teachers should encourage participation from everyone through nonverbal cues (for example, shifting gaze to nonparticipating students, nodding at them, posing the open-ended question "Would anyone else like to share?"). Eventually, the management of the group will also become the responsibility of the group. You may need to remind them of the rules of the group early on; later in the semester, students should begin to control the group on their own.

listening and perspective taking while developing increased self-esteem and awareness.

Dialogue is most powerful in attacking biases, stereotypes, and prejudices that students possess in the school setting. Dialogue should never be used to directly address bullying, because it leaves victims isolated and it is difficult not to call attention to them. Rather, dialogue is intended to provide

- Support for victims by allowing them a safe activity to participate
- Opportunities for bullies to think about their own behavior introspectively, and
- A voice for bystanders in the classroom, empowering them to become more assertive and perhaps intervene in bullying situations

The ultimate goal of the program is to promote a form of communication—dialogue—among students, and, in the process, support the development of inclusive learning and social communities.

An important step toward building an environment free from bully-victim-witness relationships is encouraging students to think about the concept of respect in the classroom using the dialogue process. See Figure 4.6 for the Respectful Classroom Exercise.

Rewarding prosocial behaviors observed in the elementary classroom setting is critical for building an environment conducive to anti-bullying initiatives. Special awards for cooperative behaviors may be distributed at school assemblies, supported by local businesses, or developed within the classroom setting through "reward bowls."

CURRICULUM: PROCESS VERSUS INFUSION

Teachers can use anti-bullying curriculum at any grade level, and teachers of every discipline may engage their students in anti-bullying programming. Traditionally, K–12 teachers use either the process approach or the infusion approach to educating students. The process curriculum approach uses a specific time of class to teach anti-bullying from a standardized curriculum. Curriculum materials specifically designed for reducing bullying behavior are discussed later in this chapter. Many violence prevention curricula also offer lessons on beating bullying behaviors in the classroom. Steps to Respect (Committee for Children, 1998) is one example of an anti-bullying curriculum designed to provide teachers with ready-made lesson plans and ideas for implementation. Teachers of all subjects (for example, health, language arts, and sciences) may engage in the process approach to anti-bullying curriculum. The stand-alone programming may be used at times, as it won't align with curricular concepts.

Figure 4.6   The Respectful Classroom

Objectives

1. To better understand the process of dialogue and reflective thinking
2. To use effective listening and empathy skills
3. To understand the importance of respect in an inclusive classroom and in constructive interpersonal relationships
4. To identify behavior and feelings of respect

Students are asked to complete the Respectful Classroom Exercise. Teachers may introduce the exercise with the following: "We have already identified what inclusive behaviors look like in the classroom. The purpose of this exercise is to identify behaviors and feelings associated with respect, an important part of building an inclusive classroom."

Respectful Classroom Exercise

Please take a few minutes to read and complete the following statements concerning respect.

I know that I am being respected when

_____

_____

_____

I know that I am not being respected when

_____

_____

_____

An example of a respectful behavior would be (Describe the behavior.)

_____

_____

_____

When I am treated with respect, I feel

_____

_____

_____

The teacher should facilitate the dialogue after the students have finished the worksheet.

Debriefing Questions

1. What came to mind when completing these statements?
2. Are there differences in the ways people experience and express respect? Similarities?
3. How might these differences impact the way we behave toward others?
4. How should we incorporate what we have learned about respect into our classroom rules?

The curriculum infusion approach involves the integration of concepts of anti-bullying and constructive conflict resolution into the existing curriculum. Primarily used by health and language arts teachers, the infusion approach requires teachers to align concepts with classroom benchmarks and standards. Lessons expose students to concepts of assertiveness, effective communication skills, perspective taking, and generating and evaluating solutions throughout lessons on language arts, science, and even math. Teachers may use a combination of techniques to best meet students' needs in the classroom. Teachers may also want to consider using other school safety content, such as violence prevention training, adding important anti-bullying components. These are usually directed toward witnesses and victims and include assertiveness and relaxation techniques. Lessons that are critical in reducing bullying behaviors in the classroom include:

- Empathy and perspective-taking skills
- Assertiveness
- Constructive conflict resolution

Teachers should also include lessons on identifying bullying behaviors, managing bully-victim incidents, and reporting incidents. A sample introductory lesson on vocabulary is provided in Figure 4.7.

Empathy and Perspective-Taking Skills

Perspective taking involves the ability to see multiple perspectives simultaneously, and empathy involves the ability to understand or sense how others feel or what they think about a situation. These skills are necessary for helping students identify how bullies, victims, and witnesses may feel during a bullying episode.

Sophisticated perspective-taking skills are related to a variety of social skills, including constructive problem solving. Students with sophisticated perspective-taking skills are better problem solvers and are more likely to generate sophisticated methods of handling difficult social situations. Therefore, students with more sophisticated, effective perspective-taking skills are more likely to empathize and are often more capable of handling conflict constructively. As a result, students skilled in empathy and perspective taking are more adept at demonstrating respectful behaviors toward others.

Robert Selman (1980) theorized that individuals progress through qualitatively different stages of perspective-taking abilities, which influence interpersonal negotiation skills. Individuals progress from developmentally unsophisticated methods of viewing interpersonal interactions to more sophisticated levels of interpersonal understanding. As humans develop, they augment their cognitive capabilities, so adults have access to a larger number of possible conflict resolution strategies than do younger children.

Figure 4.7   Vocabulary Exercise

Objectives

1. Encourage students to work together collaboratively (with unfamiliar peers).
2. Help students develop a vocabulary associated with bullying.
3. Build a foundation for a classroom approach to dealing with bullying situations.

Place the following words up on the board. Ask students to work in pairs or groups to define the words. When finished, ask the groups to write their definitions on the board next to the word. Each group should only write the definition for one word. When all the words have been defined, provide students with the following definitions to see how closely they match.

bully   An individual who uses intimidation, strength, or aggression to try to control another person

victim   An individual who suffers as a result of another's intimidation or aggression

intervene To come in between to solve a problem or stop a negative behavior or situation from continuing or occurring

witness   An individual who views or knows of a problem, behavior, or situation

taunt   To insult or tease

empathy   The ability to put oneself in someone else's shoes; to understand the thoughts and feelings of another person

ridicule   To mock or make fun of another person's speech, mannerisms, and/or clothing

---

An adaptation of the Selman model appears in Figure 4.8. As the figure depicts, young children fit developmentally into Levels 0–1 and have limited ability to understand the perspective of others, resulting in egocentric and unidirectional methods of resolving conflict. Older students fit developmentally into Levels 2–3 and possess extensive skills in understanding the perspectives of others. Collaborative methods of conflict resolution should be used by this age. Yet, students may not use these skills during bullying episodes. Often, students who make judgments based solely on their experiences or their own perceptions demonstrate poor performance of perspective-taking skills.

Teachers may find the Selman model particularly useful in developing and using cooperative learning groups for anti-bullying social skill training. For instance, educators should create cooperative learning groups composed of students of varying sophistication levels of perspective taking. Diversity of ability will enhance students with strong perspective-taking skills and will develop the use of this skill by students demonstrating developmentally inappropriate perspective-taking skills. Pairing students in Level 3 with students in Level 1 will significantly improve perspective-taking skills and will ultimately improve conflict resolution skills of Level 1 students. On the other hand, pairing Level 0 with Level 1 students is almost certain to make management of the group difficult and may increase the likelihood of destructive conflict resolution and bullying behaviors.

Figure 4.8   Interpersonal Negotiation Strategy

The following is an adaptation of Robert Selman's (1980) model of interpersonal negotiation. The age ranges are approximate and are not absolute. The levels listed are guidelines of cognitive capability and corresponding sociocognitive expectations during conflict. They suggest more of a continuum rather than absolute, mutually exclusive categories of thinking. Differences in expectations may occur, just as some flexibility of cognitive capabilities of young children occur.

Level 0: Approximate ages 3 through 6 years

Profound egocentrism marks Level 0. Children are unable to understand or appreciate fully the motivations and feelings of others. They use common conflict resolution strategies to protect the self but do not seek to maintain friendships.

Conflict resolution strategies of Level 0 include the following:

Aggression: Physical fighting, yelling, making the other person feel bad

Avoidance/withdrawal: Running away, pretending nothing is wrong

Level 1: Approximate ages 4 through 9 years

Level 1 is an improvement over Level 0 in perspective-taking skills; yet, this level is still marked by inability to understand or appreciate fully the motivations and feelings of others. Children at this developmental level do not believe that others' perspectives are of equal importance. Typically, they report that their own perspectives have greater value than other perspectives. Decisions are not based on continuing friendships. Common conflict resolution strategies demonstrated by children in this level include the following:

Giving in: Letting others have their way

Standing one's ground: "I'm right, they're wrong"

Level 2: Approximate ages 7 through 12 years

At Level 2, children have the ability to understand and appreciate the motivations and feelings of others; however, they are unable to resolve conflict situations by themselves and require third-party intervention. Common conflict resolution strategies exhibited at this level include the following:

Appealing to an authority: Asking parents or teachers to decide a conflict, flipping a coin

Compromise: Taking turns, sharing

Level 3: Approximate ages 10 to adult

At Level 3, individuals have the ability to understand and appreciate the motivations and feelings of others. They have a desire to maintain a relationship with the disputing partner and do not require third-party intervention. Common conflict resolution strategies demonstrated at this level include the following:

Collaboration: Negotiation, creating solutions that accommodate needs of both disputants

Activities that allow students to demonstrate how their biases and prejudgments affect their behavior toward others are useful, particularly at the high school level. Figures 4.9 and 4.10 are sample exercises demonstrating how students make assumptions about others and how these assumptions affect behavior. The existence and performance of sophisticated perspective taking enhances the likelihood that students will empathize when witnessing bullying or serving as the bully or victim.

Figure 4.9   Letts/Nots Cultures Exercise (for Middle School Students)

Purpose: The exercise demonstrates how individuals make assumptions about others with limited information, and how these impact one's behavior toward others.

Directions: Divide students into two groups, labeling one group the Letts Culture and the other group the Nots Culture. Be sure to include both bullies and their victims in the same culture group. Provide each group with a list of only their culture's characteristics. Separate the groups for 10 minutes. During this time, students should practice the characteristics of their culture. After 10 minutes, the Letts and Nots cultures will meet for the first time. The goal of each group is to interact with the other culture and try to learn as much about them as possible through their behaviors. Group members are not allowed to inform the other group of their "written" characteristics.

Discussion Questions

1. Ask the Nots Culture to describe the characteristics of the Letts Culture.
2. Ask the Letts Culture to describe the characteristics of the Nots Culture.
3. How did you learn about the cultures?

Allow each group to read the written characteristics of the other group before asking each group the next set of questions.

1. In what ways were you correct or incorrect? What assumptions did you make about the other group that were correct or incorrect?
2. How do incorrect assumptions affect the way you interact with one another?
3. What might you do to make sure you are not making incorrect assumptions about others?
4. How does this exercise relate to the way you interact with each other in the classroom or at home?

Characteristics of the Letts Culture

- Letts are extremely agreeable.
- Letts enjoy talking and discussing issues (often loudly).
- Letts love the outdoors and enjoy natural sunlight.
- Letts like to move around and rarely stand in one place at any one time.
- Letts make eye contact frequently with others.
- Letts stand closely to persons upon meeting them.
- Letts often interrupt each other when they talk.

Characteristics of the Nots Culture

- Nots allow others to finish speaking before talking.
- Nots prefer to stand some distance from others upon meeting them.
- Nots dislike eye contact with others.
- Nots prefer activities requiring little movement.
- Nots prefer the indoors and like to stay out of the sun.
- Nots do not talk often and when they do talk it is in a soft voice.
- Nots often disagree with the opinions of others.

For younger students, empathy may be learned through exercises that promote commonalities. Younger children who learn similarities between and among themselves and others are going to be less likely to demonstrate bullying behaviors and will be more likely to intervene as witnesses in bullying situations. The activity shown in Figure 4.11 assists elementary school children with better understanding others by understanding themselves first.

Figure 4.10   Trading Places Exercise (for High School Students)

Purpose: The goal of this exercise is to provide students with an opportunity to explore their own stereotypes and biases, which may ultimately impact their behavior toward others. The exercise also highlights how individuals make assumptions about others using very limited information.

Directions: Provide students with Round 1. Ask students to rank each of the eleven individuals according to the extent to which the student would trade places with the individual for one year. A rank of (1) would reflect the most appealing trade and (11) the least appealing trade. Once students have completed the worksheet for Round 1, ask them to turn the sheet over, so they cannot see their rankings. Provide students with Round 2, and repeat the instructions for completion. Once finished with Round 2, students should hide their responses before completing Round 3.

Discussion Questions

1. What was your most appealing trade? Least appealing? Why?

2. How did your rankings change across the three rounds?

3. On what criteria did you base your rankings?

4. Why did your ranking change across the rounds?

5. How is this exercise applicable to everyday life in the classroom?

6. How do assumptions based on incomplete information affect our interactions with one another?

Round 1   *Rank*

  1. 61-year-old white male aerospace manager   _____

  2. Successful owner/operator of beauty salon   _____

  3. Black female (pregnant) with three children   _____

  4. Native American Chief and board member of the National Organization   _____
      of Native Americans

  5. Colorful, loosely attired Hispanic female   _____

  6. 26-year-old black male working at McDonald's; scar on left side of face   _____

  7. Blind, panhandling homeless person   _____

  8. Asian merchant walking home at 3:00 a.m.   _____

  9. 45-year-old male auto worker   _____

10. 37-year-old female bank president   _____

11. 12-year-old child prodigy (piano)   _____

Figure 4.10 (Continued)

		Rank
Round 2		
1. 61-year-old white male aerospace manager	Two (2) granddaughters; recently divorced	_____
2. Successful owner/operator of beauty salon	Single male parent of 2-year-old son	_____
3. Black female (pregnant) with three children	Husband died in Desert Storm (Captain)	_____
4. Native American Chief and board member of the National Organization of Native Americans	Bejeweled and falsely arrested three times	_____
5. Colorful, loosely attired Hispanic female	Works out of her home	_____
6. 26-year-old black male working at McDonald's; scar on left side of face	Part-time university student	_____
7. Blind, panhandling homeless person	Lost sight in gang war	_____
8. Asian merchant walking home at 3:00 a.m.	Three daughters attending NYU	_____
9. 45-year-old male auto worker	Married with two children	_____
10. 37-year-old female bank president	Recently underwent major surgery leading to long process of recovery	_____
11. 12-year-old child prodigy (piano)	Played at Carnegie Hall at age of 7	_____

Round 3   *Rank*

1. 61-year-old
   white male
   aerospace manager

   Two (2) grand-
   daughters; recently
   divorced

   Recently arrested
   for stealing   _____

2. Successful owner/
   operator of beauty salon

   Single male parent
   of 2-year-old son

   Gay male   _____

3. Black female (pregnant)
   with three children

   Husband died in
   Desert Storm
   (Captain)

   Nuclear physicist;
   graduate of MIT   _____

4. Native American Chief
   and board member of the
   National Organization of
   Native Americans

   Bejeweled and
   falsely arrested
   three times

   Convicted of
   gambling and
   prostitution   _____

5. Colorful, loosely attired
   Hispanic female

   Works out of
   her home

   President and owner   _____
   of architectural firm

6. 26-year-old black
   male working at
   McDonald's.
   Scar on left side of face.

   Part-time
   university
   student

   Owner of
   numerous   _____
   McDonald's locations

7. Blind panhandling
   homeless person

   Lost sight in
   gang war

   Shot as innocent
   passenger in
   drive-by shooting   _____

8. Asian merchant
   walking home at
   3.00 a.m.

   Three daughters
   attending NYU

   Runs store front for
   drug operation   _____

9. 45-year-old male
   auto worker

   Married with two
   children

   Recently won $25
   million in lottery and
   quit work   _____

10. 37-year-old female
    bank president

    Recently underwent
    major surgery
    leading to long
    recovery process

    Will soon be
    marrying female
    companion   _____

11. 12-year-old child
    prodigy (piano)

    Played at Carnegie
    Hall at age of 7

    Contracted AIDS
    from a blood
    transfusion   _____

Figure 4.11   Empathy Exercise (for Elementary School Children)

Children Like *Us*

- Read to the students the book *Children Just Like Me*, by Barnabas and Anabel Kindersley (ISBN: 0-8136-6265-6). The photographs and text depict the homes, schools, family life, and culture of young people around the world. Children from more than 31 countries are interviewed, with their stories recorded in the book.

- Assign students to work in pairs. Have students complete the student worksheet by interviewing their partner.

- Once students finish the interview, the teacher may discuss similarities and differences with regard to food, games, and family events among the students' own families.

- Tell students that the class will be creating a "Children Just Like Me" book containing each student's photograph and stories. The students' interviews will serve as the basis for the classroom book.

- After the class book is completed, discuss what a reader of the classroom book would learn from the stories and photographs. What are the similarities? Differences?

<u>Student Worksheet</u>

Student Name:

Interviewer Name:

Family Background (number of brother/sisters, aunts/uncles)

Favorite Food

Favorite Movie/Television Program

Favorite Things to Do With Family

Favorite Place to Be

Favorite Toy/Game

Favorite Book

Assertiveness

Assertiveness training education is important as a classroom instruction topic to reduce bullying behavior because it targets not just victimized students. Rather, assertiveness training is critical in developing witnesses' skills and creating attitudes toward the bullying behaviors of others that tend to reduce the incidence of bullying. Stevens, deBourdeaudhuij, and Van Oost (2000) cited that younger children benefit from assertiveness training that focuses on active listening skills and giving support to victims of bullying, whereas assertiveness toward aggressors is better adapted to older students. Identified goals of assertiveness training are presented in Figure 4.12.

Assertiveness is the act of an individual standing up for his or her own rights in a situation without violating the rights of another individual. Assertive responses may be either verbal or nonverbal. Assertiveness is a required skill for bullied students because it will assist them in responding to the bully, stating their position, emotions, and wishes clearly and directly. The assertive witness may also defend the victimized student or may challenge the behavior of the bully. The assertive student is usually resistant to manipulation by the bully and resistant to the bully's aggressive tendencies.

Students may learn assertive verbal responses through effective communication skills. Teaching students to communicate effectively with each other will help students resolve much of their conflict. Effective communication skills will help victims and witnesses of bullying episodes manage, intervene, and even prevent bullying behaviors. One strategy for communicating effectively is through the use of "I-messages." I-messages assist individuals with identifying the main issues of a conflict situation. Usually, when anger is present conflict participants make "you-statements" such as "You always . . . !" Or "You are such a . . . !" You-statements are frequently used in bullying situations that are relational or verbally abusive. Such you-statements are hostile comments intended to inflict harm. Students instead should be encouraged to practice "I-statements" to support assertive techniques and counteract the harmful "you-statements."

Figure 4.12   Goals of Assertiveness Training

When teaching assertiveness, the goal is to teach students how to:
- Make assertive statements
- Resist manipulations and perceived threats associated with bullying
- Respond to bullying behavior
- Enlist the support of bystanders

I-messages possess three general components (Gordon, 1970) and may contain a fourth component that is particularly useful in confronting bullying situations. These components include:

1. A statement of the speaker's feelings (for example, "I feel . . .")

2. A description of the noxious behavior that provoked the feelings (for example, "when you . . .")

3. The reason that the behavior affects the individual ("because . . .")

4. A behavior that would alleviate the stated emotion ("I would like you to . . .")

I-messages may serve as the basis for victims and witnesses responding to bullying situations. An example of an I-message might be, "I feel angry when you call me that name because it isn't respectful (nice), and it isn't my name. I would like you to call me Calvin." Another example would be, "I feel sad when you pick on Jennifer because she is minding her own business. I would like you to include her in the game."

While assertiveness training is taught, bullies in the classroom will also be trained. Therefore, it is very important to infuse the techniques of assertiveness with conflict resolution strategy techniques such as role-playing and modeling. See Figure 4.13 for a strategy for teaching assertiveness.

Figure 4.14 highlights some guidelines regarding the use of role-plays for teaching assertiveness to combat bullying in the classroom setting. Certainly, role-playing should be used only by teachers who have carefully

Figure 4.13   Assertion Skill Exercise

Objectives

1. Provide students with an opportunity to practice assertiveness statements.
2. Encourage students to role-play using masks.
3. Develop skills of witnesses to intervene in bullying situations.
4. Begin to develop a sense of community and safety within the classroom.

Have each student create a mask for assertion skills practices. Wearing masks will often equalize students in the classroom and will enable victims to participate in the exercise without fear of consequences. The mask should represent student's own personality and should not be based on a character from television or popular culture. If students are struggling with their masks, ask them to take the first letter of their name and match it with an emotion. Draw the mask face showing that emotion. This will also provide students with practice in naming and drawing emotions beyond mad, sad, or happy.

Once the masks have been completed, have students practice "I-messages" as a means of practicing effective communication skills and supporting assertion techniques. Provide opportunities for students to use the masks over a period of time and even in role-play situations. Gradually eliminate the use of the masks and continue to provide opportunities for students to practice their assertion techniques.

Figure 4.14   Role-Play Guidelines

- Ask open-ended questions that promote discussion such as the examples that follow.
- Demonstrate feedback skills during the exercise using specific examples and statements.
- Reinforce students who provide constructive feedback.
- Ask the actors:
    1. How did you feel playing the role?
    2. What nonverbal cues were you demonstrating?
    3. How did the other person respond to your actions and words?
- Ask the observers:
    1. How did you feel as you watched your peers participate in the role-play exercise? (The purpose of this question is to begin a discussion regarding witnessing and intervening in bullying situations. Students might respond that they felt frustrated with the situation, angry at the bully, or pleased with the victim's response to the bullying behavior.)
    2. What stands out about the behavior of the student playing the victim?
    3. What might the student playing the victim do differently in the future? How might these changes affect the outcome of the interaction?

conducted an assessment of bully-victim relationships in the class, so as to avoid reinforcing bullying behaviors through role-playing. Specifically, teachers should avoid casting a bully in the bully role and a victim in the victim role. Role-playing is not only useful for teaching perspective taking and empathy, but is beneficial to victims for honing assertiveness skills. Figure 4.15 outlines several role-play options for use in the classroom.

Both elementary and secondary students will benefit from identifying methods for intervening in bullying situations. The more opportunities students have to practice situations and prepare for the outcomes, the more likely students will engage in intervening behaviors. Students may provide content for role-plays by completing the form presented in Figure 4.16.

Constructive Conflict Resolution Strategies

Bullies and victims will benefit from constructive conflict resolution education, which teaches children to replace competitive with collaborative methods of resolution. As discussed previously, bullies and victims demonstrate highly competitive conflict resolution strategies during their interactions. Bullies use aggressive methods, and victims avoid or withdraw from conflict. In both cases of aggression and withdrawal, participants resolve conflicts using win-loss solutions. Bullies perceive that the use of aggression as a means of resolution results in "winning" while victims, through withdrawal, "lose."

The goal, therefore, of teaching constructive conflict resolution strategies is to provide students with skills, knowledge, and attitudes to resolve

Figure 4.15   Role-Play Suggestions

Situation A

STUDENT 1: You are standing by your locker and are suddenly bumped from behind. You are hit so hard that you drop your books in the hall.

STUDENT 2: Your teacher just finished hassling you about missed homework, again! You see a favorite target (Student 1) in the hallway and go out of your way to throw your body into the locker.

Situation B

STUDENT 1: You are just returning to school after being suspended for fighting in the gym during P.E. class. You finally gave Student 2 what he deserved, as you have endured name calling, physical aggression, and even homework stealing. The last straw was when he called you a name when you missed an important shot during a basketball game. The principal only gave him a verbal warning, but you were suspended for fighting. You are really angry.

STUDENT 2: Student 1 is such a tattle-tale and is constantly in your face. The only way to keep him away from you and your friends is to ride him a bit by name calling. You weren't doing anything wrong during the basketball game when he came charging at you. You needed two stitches.

Situation C

STUDENT 1: You overhear a comment made by Sara, a classmate, that a popular boy is going to ask you to a party. You don't know the boy well, but would eagerly accept an invitation. You receive a note to meet him in a classroom after school. When you arrive, no one is there. You discover it was a cruel joke.

STUDENT 2: You have known Student 1 since first grade, but your paths at school do not cross frequently. Student 1 started to hang out with a boy you are interested in pursuing.

---

conflict using collaborative methods. Principles of constructive conflict resolution education are listed in Figure 4.17.

As depicted in Figure 4.18, children participate in conflicts that originate from issues of property, status or power, and ideology. Topics of conflict are developmental; young children engage in conflicts over sources different from those that engage adolescents and adults. These age-related differences are due to a number of factors, including the changing nature of friendship patterns in children and the way that cognitive capabilities for thinking about and processing information evolve during childhood.

Children in the elementary grades are more likely to have conflicts with others over issues such as property and space. Frequently, young children will have conflicts over possession of a toy or swing or another person's attention. Although adolescents have been known to oppose each other about space issues, they are more likely to clash over differences of values or beliefs, particularly with classmates. During the upper elementary grades and middle school years, children begin to engage in conflict over issues of power or hierarchy and status. Peer conflict in this age group often focuses on isolation and highlighting differences among children.

Figure 4.16   Sample Bullying Incident Role-Play Form

Date: _____

Names and grade levels of students involved in the bullying incident (important in that these students are not to be selected to role-play the situation):

Where did the incident occur?   What did the incident involve?

_____ Classroom   _____ Name Calling

_____ Hallway   _____ Pushing/Shoving

_____ Cafeteria   _____ Teasing

_____ Outside   _____ Isolating

_____ Other   _____ Other

When did this occur?
Briefly describe the bullying incident.

Role-Playing Content: How do you wish the role-play to look? If description above is incomplete, improvise the role-play. (Check all that apply.)

Incident outcome: Intervention by:

_____ Victim uses "I-messages"   _____ Student witnesses

_____ Bully retreats   _____ Adult (student's teacher)

_____ Victim retreats   _____ Adult (other)

_____ Intervention   _____ No witness intervention

_____ Other (specify) _____

Figure 4.17   Principles of Constructive Conflict Resolution Education

1. *Identification of the problem:* Support students' ability to identify the problem and express it in terms of both conflict participants.
2. *Expression of each person's feelings:* Identify conflict participants' feelings, both the protagonist's and the antagonist's.
3. *Description of strategies for resolving the conflict:* Develop strategies that address the needs of both conflict participants.
4. *Evaluation of conflict resolution strategies:* Veto solutions that do not address the problem or the needs of each of the conflict participants.

Figure 4.18   Sources of Interpersonal Conflict

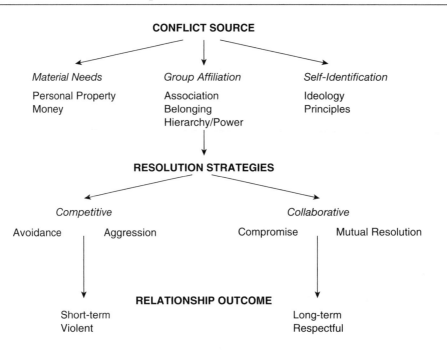

These different sources of conflict will more likely lead to different strategies of conflict resolution. Developmentally, children begin to use more sophisticated methods of conflict resolution because of the changing nature of friendship patterns and their developing cognitive capabilities for processing information. Children who oppose each other due to issues of space and property (fighting over a ball or a book) tend to resolve the conflict using competitive methods (physical aggression or giving in). This type of conflict resolution is less likely with children in a dispute over ideological or belief systems (for example, disparity over preference of sports teams). Young children are more likely to use competitive methods of conflict resolution because they are unable to think in a highly abstract manner and because sustainability of friendships is not a priority. Unlike early elementary school children, adolescents have the cognitive capabilities to resolve all conflict using sophisticated methods. However, they still possess unsophisticated methods mastered in the early years because conflict resolution skills are augmented as children develop; early skills are added to, not replaced. Adolescents are more likely, however, to attempt to collaborate on a resolution to conflict because they highly value maintaining friendships.

Children in the middle school years who engage in conflicts involving hierarchy or power and status differences tend to resolve these conflicts in destructive ways. For conflict in which participants perceive differences in status or power, competitive conflict resolution strategies—such as avoidance or withdrawal, giving in, and aggression—are common responses.

In many schools, educators use cooperative learning activities to introduce the concepts of constructive conflict resolution (Johnson & Johnson, 1995b). Deutsch (1993) stated that cooperative learning groups are an excellent mechanism for teaching these skills because they require positive interdependence, face-to-face interactions, and individual accountability. However, cooperative learning groups are often misused in social skill training development. Too often, educators will attempt to combine a social skill lesson with one with an academic goal. Rather, cooperative learning groups must be used for purposes of social skill development or learning an academic concept, but not both. The composition of the cooperative learning group determines the benefit to the group. Therefore, cooperative learning groups that are developed for the purpose of teaching a social skill, such as constructive conflict resolution, require group members with a variety of abilities. Too often, bullies and their victims are placed together in cooperative learning groups, without regard to the similar way in which they resolve conflict. Cooperative learning groups composed of bullies and victims will merely learn to reinforce the negative way they resolve conflict as opposed to learning more sophisticated methods. When determining members of cooperative learning groups, identify students' social skills ability rather than their academic ability. Place highly functioning members with lower-functioning students so that highly functioning students may serve as models and mentors of sophisticated problem-solving methods. Students who may require assistance with social skills should be placed with students demonstrating higher ability. A method for measuring social skill ability is discussed in Chapter 6.

Some ideas for teaching constructive conflict resolution skills are presented in Figure 4.19.

Figure 4.19   Infusing Conflict Resolution Skills Into the Curriculum

---

1. Have students develop journals in which they record conflicts that occur in their lives and the lives of others. How were the conflicts resolved, how could they have been resolved, and how would different solutions create different results?

2. Have students identify conflicts in television and media and through newspapers. Have students record the number of times participants use constructive conflict resolution strategies. Develop graphs outlining numbers or percentages of various types of conflict resolution strategies and their outcomes. Identify other methods that conflict participants use, and create new, more constructive ways of resolving the conflict.

3. Role-play conflicts occurring in the classroom. Have students generate solutions and role-play each possible outcome. Be sure to have students reflect on the feelings of each of the participants. Role-play ideas can be generated through an "idea box" placed in the front of the room. Review the role-play suggestions before engaging the classroom to determine their appropriateness. Be sure to role-play different types of conflicts including student-student, student-teacher, parent-child, and sibling conflict in order to assist students with generalizing their skills to multiple relationships.

Classroom Curriculum to Prevent Bullying: The Process Approach

Classroom curricula for anti-bullying efforts have become popular, yet empirical support for these programs is limited. In addition, many programs focus on physical and verbal bullying and do not include sexual or relational bullying (Walker et al., 1998). As well, anti-bullying curricula are more often geared toward elementary school students rather than secondary students. A number of examples of anti-bullying curriculum are currently available for use in the classroom.

Bully Proofing Your School: A Comprehensive Approach for Elementary Schools (Garrity et al., 2000) provides a comprehensive blueprint for implementing a bully-proofing program designed to make school environments safe for children both physically and psychologically. The book recommends schoolwide approaches as well as mechanisms for training students in the classroom setting. The student curriculum is designed to be completed within 2–3 months and emphasizes ways for teachers to develop the skills of victims and witnesses while changing the behaviors of bullies.

Steps to Respect: A Bullying Prevention Program (Committee for Children, 1998) is a school-based social and emotional learning program designed to decrease bullying behaviors and help children build more respectful, caring peer relationships. The program begins by teaching children friendship skills, and then continues by teaching children how to recognize bullying, how to assertively refuse bullying, and how to report bullying to adults.

Quit It! A Teacher's Guide on Teasing and Bullying (Frosche, Sprung, & Mullin-Rindler, 1998) contains lesson plans for children ages 5–8 years. Class discussions, role-plays, creative drawing, and physical games provide the framework for understanding the differences between teasing and bullying.

CLASSROOM PROGRAMS TO PREVENT BULLYING

In addition to selecting and teaching an anti-bullying curriculum, teachers can implement several programs at the classroom level to teach students to resolve conflicts peacefully. The Positive Behavior Intervention and Support Program (PBS) and the "peace table" are two successful programs that work at the classroom level to reduce the incidence of bullying behavior.

Positive Behavior Intervention and Support Program

The Positive Behavioral Intervention and Support Program is one mechanism useful for changing the climate of the classroom and thus, the prevalence of bullying behaviors. An empirically proven program, PBS promotes improvements in teachers' instructional styles, classroom routines, and settings to develop more harmonious and effective learning environments (Taylor-Greene et al., 1997). The program requires a collaborative approach between families and professionals to alter problem behaviors and create support systems for students (Todd, Horner, & Sugai, 1999). Although used primarily for violence reduction efforts in schools, PBS is being evaluated for its direct implications on anti-bullying efforts.

Peace Table

The peace table process is used more frequently with younger students (second grade and below) than with older students. Preferably, a round, low table is placed in the back of the classroom. Teachers discuss the meaning of conflict and hurt feelings. They instruct students in a conflict situation to go to the peace table to resolve their conflict. It is intended that teachers are to facilitate the peace table; students place their hands on the table one at a time and are allowed to tell their story. Teachers encourage students to generate possible solutions one at a time, using the table as a physical reminder of turn taking during the problem-solving process.

SUMMARY

Teachers can manage bullying behaviors in their classrooms in several ways. Most important, they need to be prepared. They must be able to recognize bullying, in all its forms, and they must know in advance what techniques they will use to diffuse a negative situation between students should one arise. Preparation allows teachers to anticipate sources of friction between students, prevent them when possible, and respond to them appropriately when necessary.

Educating the students is the other key to creating a respectful classroom and preventing bullying behaviors. Students can be taught to empathize with others, to respond assertively, and to engage in constructive problem solving when disagreements arise. By encouraging potential bullies to take another perspective and teaching potential victims how to be more assertive, teachers can reduce the incidence of bullying and build a more cooperative classroom for all students.

5

Strategies for Intervention

INTERVENING IN
BULLY-VICTIM RELATIONSHIPS

Bullying episodes may occur in the classroom despite efforts to develop and implement an anti-bullying environment. Intervention strategies must then be enacted. Although somewhat similar to management strategies, intervention techniques are intended to go beyond management, by providing support and education for anti-bullying initiatives. Educating bullies and their victims is a natural by-product of effective intervention techniques.

The effectiveness of intervention strategies varies, as does the perceived usefulness of intervening in bullying situations without having prevention and management techniques in place. Few researchers have studied how intervention strategies alone affect the bully-victim-witness relationship in comparison with intervention strategies used in conjunction with a classroom approach to prevention and management. One might speculate that using intervention strategies in isolation is not as effective in reducing the likelihood of future bullying behaviors as using intervention strategies within a classroom or whole school approach.

Figure 5.1   Strategies for Intervention

- Intervene in bullying situations quickly and resolutely.
- Consistently apply consequences every time you are witness to bullying.
- Reinforce behaviors when bystanders defuse bullying.

Practitioners also disagree as to how to intervene in bullying situations and how to involve victims with consequences directed toward the bully, if rendered. Limited empirical research is available to support techniques for intervention and to answer questions of how, when, and why specific intervention techniques might be effective.

Intervention strategies, like management techniques, require teachers to prepare for a variety of bullying situations in which they may need to intervene. Teachers and school leaders must be prepared, for instance, to intervene in bullying situations occurring in the classroom, in the hallway, or on the playground. As well, the numbers of bullies, victims, and witnesses are important characteristics to consider when intervening. Finally, the type of bullying occurring (physical, verbal, or relational) is relevant to strategies for intervention. Regardless of the context of the bullying situation, several clear intervention strategies are required when teachers witness bullying. A list of strategies is provided in Figure 5.1.

Step 1: Intervening

The first step in intervention is to take immediate action to stop the behaviors of the bully. If the bully is physically aggressing toward the victim, call for another adult to assist. Many large schools institute a buddy system for teachers, pairing geographically close teachers together to address issues of school safety. Until another adult is available, be sure to clear the area of other students, yet remain close to the bully and victim. It is important to position yourself so that your body remains perpendicular to both the bully and the victim. Do not turn your back to the victim, because this pose creates the perception that the victim requires defending. Standing in this fashion is important because it establishes that blaming will not occur during the interaction. This positioning also protects the person intervening from potential threats of aggression from the victim, bully, or supporters.

When physical or verbal aggression is involved, step into the situation and clearly and succinctly announce that the behavior is to stop. Following this imperative, instruct the students involved in the bullying situation on next steps (for example, sitting at a desk, standing by a door) as a means of defusing the situation. Deliver verbal cues in a firm voice, but do not raise your voice or use a hostile tone. In cases of physical and verbal bullying, it is important that the teacher remain in the area until the behavior has ended; it is ineffective to insist that the behavior stop and then leave before it actually does.

The first step of intervention must be handled with great finesse, as a harsh or authoritarian response to the bullying may validate the treatment demonstrated by the bully toward the victim. Witnesses may also view the harsh response and model the behavior, or they may become vindictive toward the teacher or the victim. It is important that teachers do not display anger or aggression themselves when intervening, as this may result in classroom management issues for the teachers in the future if bullies take out their revenge in the classroom setting. In some instances, teachers' or administrators' heightened response to the bullying may actually mobilize the bully supporters and in turn reduce intervening behaviors by witnesses.

Often, bullying episodes will occur during classroom instruction. Rules for intervening in the classroom are similar to those for intervening on the playground or in the hallway. Teachers should place themselves near the bully and victim to end the physical altercation and firmly announce that the behavior is to stop. Verbal bullying should be stopped immediately with a firm, resolute tone and a message such as "This behavior is unacceptable and will stop now."

Step 2: The Mini-Conference

Once the behavior has stopped, a mini-conference should occur as the second step in the intervention. This second step of intervention will differ somewhat depending on the venue of the situation. Mini-conferences will have to be approached differently if the incident occurs in the classroom as opposed to in the hallway or on the playground.

If incidents occur in the classroom, the bullying behavior must be dealt with immediately and not deflected in order to continue with classroom instruction. Ignoring incidents in the classroom validates the behavior. The mini-conference, however, should not take place in the classroom setting. Waiting for a convenient time, such as lunch or after school, may be appropriate; however, the bully and victim are best served if the conference occurs as close to the incident as possible, so that bullies clearly understand the connection between their actions and the consequences. Conducting the mini-conference in class is not appropriate, because it provides the bully a welcome audience for the victim's pain.

Bullying behavior that occurs on the playground or in the hallways may be addressed in a mini-conference immediately. Witnesses and supporters should be excused from the area so that the main bully and victim may be addressed privately.

Figure 5.2   Mini-Conference Strategies

The mini-conference should include the following:
- Affirmation that the bullying behavior is out in the open
- Identification of the behavior of the bully as wrong
- Deliberation of consequences for the behavior
- Demonstration that the teacher will maintain channels of communication for both the bully and victim in the future

---

The mini-conference should occur with the bully and the victim present and in as private a location as possible. The mini-conference should contain the components outlined in Figure 5.2.

An important first step in the mini-conference is affirming that the bullying behavior is out in the open. Bullying behaviors are most effective because they are often conducted in secrecy. Affirming that these behaviors are acknowledged will ease some of the anxiety of the victim and will place the bully on notice that the behaviors will be watched in the future. The affirmation should be stated in a reassuring tone toward both the bully and the victim because the bullying behavior is a problem for both individuals. In some cases, the affirmation will relieve the bully, who might be seeking assistance with his or her behavior.

Identifying the behavior as wrong is the next component of the mini-conference. The person leading the conference should describe the exact behavior rather than make a global statement about the bully. For instance, say, "Pushing another student onto the concrete is wrong." It is not effective to say, "Johnny, you were really bad." Do not connect the bully and the victim in the mini-conference when identifying the behavior, and do not add emotions. For instance, the statement, "Johnny, you really hurt Sam when you pushed him down" places the teacher in a blame-defense mode that will alienate both the bully and the victim. In addition, the teacher may not be accurately reflecting the way that Sam feels. This statement merely reinforces Johnny's desire to hurt Sam, and it does not identify the behavior as wrong.

It is important that the bully and the victim both then model the teacher's example by identifying the behavior as wrong. The bully and the victim should both state a similar phrase to each other about the behavior. Bullies need to say their behavior is wrong as a mechanism to begin to think and know that the behavior is wrong. The bully's power over the victim is diffused through the admission. In addition, victims benefit by modeling the statement because it provides them with practice in asserting themselves against the bullying behavior.

Deliberation of consequences is the next component of the mini-conference. If districtwide policies and school procedures have been

Figure 5.3   Examples of Consequences for Bullying

For Elementary School Students

- Missing recess. Student must help clean up the playground or classroom.
- Staying after school to help clean up the playground or classroom.
- Creating a presentation on bullying, including posters or flyers and distributing them to a younger grade.
- Writing a report on a peacemaker and presenting it to the class.
- Helping the teacher develop or maintain the kindness program in the school. Student can help with record keeping.

For Secondary Students

- Assisting with the development of a bullying hot spot map and then providing assistance with supervising in these areas of the school
- Developing schoolwide events to launch the anti-bullying programs through school television or assemblies
- Making presentations at parent/guardian meetings on bullying
- Interviewing mental health professionals on the effects of bullying
- Forming "friendship groups" for students of younger grades

---

implemented, then the deliberation of consequences may involve merely an announcement of the consequences. In situations where teachers have some discretion as to the consequences, the mini-conference is one way to have both the bully and the victim generate strategies together to handle the situation. Begin by outlining the types of consequences that should occur as a result of the bullying behavior. Consequences should involve possible prosocial outcomes. Examples of consequences are listed in Figure 5.3. Have the bully and victim generate consequences together and have them agree. Bullies are less likely to retaliate for the consequences if they take part in the decision-making process. Victims are also helped because they are empowered to decide repercussions for the behavior with the bully, and, at least momentarily, a power shift occurs between the bully and the victim.

The final step in the mini-conference involves the teacher establishing that the mini-conference is merely a first step in the process of ending the bullying behavior. The teacher should outline the next steps in the process, which will include individual conferences with the students and observation and record keeping of behaviors demonstrated by both the victim and the bully. If possible, the teacher should identify when and where the individual conferences will occur.

Teachers should not ask for apologies for the behavior at this time. Students who have been victimized will not appreciate or believe the apology (or handshake), and bullies will deliver the apology only because they are asked to do so. Apologies may be extended only after the individual conferences are held.

Step 3: Individual Conferences

Each of the bullying participants will require individual conferences soon after the bullying event and the mini-conference. The goal of individual conferences is to speak directly to each of the participants about the behaviors that place them at risk for bully-victim relationships.

Bullies

Conferences with students who expressed the bullying behavior should directly address their errors in thinking about victimization. The conference should include:

- A statement that the bullying behaviors are wrong
- An explanation of why the behaviors are wrong and what their effects are, and
- A description of ways to change the behaviors

Students will need to hear again that the bullying behaviors are wrong; teachers should be certain to express this without defending the victim or blaming the bully. A statement that the behavior will not be tolerated is also important during the individual conference with the bully. Ask the bully to think about and identify why he or she is engaging in the bullying behavior. Again, be sure to focus on the behavior and not the victim. The bully may state, "Peg is just so skinny and ugly." In response, quickly clarify that your question is why the bully felt the need to name-call. Insist that any characteristic or aspect of the victim is not to be mentioned. This is an important step toward separating the behavior of the bully from that of the victim.

Next, the impact of the bullying behaviors should be discussed. The impact on the victim should be minimized. Rather, discuss how bullying behaviors are unacceptable in adulthood or in other social situations with peers. Identify the impact of the behaviors on other people, including the teacher, parents, siblings, and other students. Ask the student to identify how other students might view the behavior and how friendship patterns are formed.

Finally, educate bullies on how to ask for help. Provide the student with ways to communicate to you (verbally or nonverbally) that he or she is thinking of engaging in bullying behaviors and explain how the teacher and student may work together to intervene. Describe methods for calming down or identifying anger cues that may precede the bullying and ways in which to manage the anger. Brainstorm positive strategies that may be used in place of bullying behaviors.

Victims

Students who have been victimized will require assistance following the mini-conference. Teachers will need to engage the victims with an empathetic, supportive style in order to establish or maintain the channels of communication. Conferences with the victimized students should include the clear message that the behavior of the bully was wrong and should not be duplicated. Teachers should also describe how victims might handle the behaviors and bullying situations in the future.

As with students who bully, victimized students must know that the bullying behavior is wrong. Teachers must be careful to reduce victim blame by clearly identifying the behaviors as inappropriate and unacceptable in the classroom, in school, and even into adulthood.

Teachers should then move to providing victimized students with strategies for preventing the behaviors from occurring in the future and managing the behaviors if they do occur. Identify methods for record keeping about bullying behaviors. Provide the student with guidelines for recording times, places, dates, and descriptions of bullying behaviors. This activity will empower the student and will assist the teacher in possible future consequences or necessary programming changes. Ways to prevent the bullying should also be identified, such as staying close to friends or an adult during lunch, during recess, or while changing classes. Talk about finding someone to assist the student during a bullying episode. If the person doesn't help, the student should tell someone else, such as a parent, another teacher, sibling, or student.

Next, management of the bullying situation should be discussed. Brainstorm ways to respond to the bullying behavior. Be clear that responses should be directed at the behavior and not the person. Practice "I-messages" specific to common situations. Students should be warned not to seek revenge by fighting or engaging in bullying behaviors themselves. Provide them with a simple mechanism for managing the situation. A sample is provided in Figure 5.4.

Witnesses and Supporters

Witnesses and supporters play an important role in the bullying episode, as they are in a position to intervene and end the behavior or to encourage the continuation of the behavior. Teachers should conference with witnesses of the bullying behavior if it is possible to identify the students. Teachers and school leaders should pay close attention to students who are likely to intervene in the future during bullying situations. The purpose of the conference is simple: to encourage the students to intervene in bullying situations. Students should be asked to follow this procedure:

1. Report bullying behavior as quickly as possible to an adult. Provide a clear message that bullying behavior is wrong and unacceptable in the school and in the classroom. Identify differences between tattling and reporting bullying behavior. Discuss how students

Figure 5.4   Managing the Bullying Situation

- Ignore the bullying behavior when possible. *Ignore* does not mean *forget*.
- Be assertive, use "I-messages," and tell bullies you wish them to stop the behavior.
- Physically distance yourself from the bullying behavior.
- Ask for assistance from other peers or adults.

shouldn't be afraid of reporting, and recognize the fear of reprisal and mechanisms that are in place for ensuring confidentiality.

2. Intervene (when possible) in the bullying situation by clearly stating, in a firm voice, that the behavior is wrong. Talk about how witnesses (even when they don't join in the behavior) assist bullies with their behaviors. Brainstorm with students what they should say to bullies and how they should deliver the statements.

3. Identify ways to prevent the bullying behaviors from occurring. Brainstorm ways that the students may assist victims and bullies in the classroom or on the playground.

Step 4: Record Keeping

Once the mini-conference and individual conferences are completed, the next task is intervention record keeping. It is important for teachers and school leaders to begin extensive record keeping on the bullying situation. The records will track the progress of the intervention and assist the teacher in considering other classroom prevention programming.

Teachers and school leaders should consider recording all observations and reports of incidents of bullying to see if a pattern emerges. Important patterns might include times of the day, locations, and whether particular students are engaged in bullying or victimization.

See Figure 5.5 for a sample record-keeping report form. The record-keeping report form results may be useful for individual conferences with students, both bullies and victims. For instance, the record-keeping report form completed by teachers or school leaders may be compared with reports maintained by the bully or victim. The comparison process is particularly helpful, as it may provide insight to teachers about the quality of their observations and extent of the problem perceived by the victims. In some instances, the comparison of records will serve an important lesson, as ineffectual bullies and victims often perceive all negative peer interactions inaccurately as bullying behaviors. Teachers may use these data discrepancies to reinforce the differences in bullying behaviors as compared to destructive and negative peer behaviors.

Figure 5.5   Sample Record Keeping Form for Teachers

Date _____

Time _____

Duration or length of episode:

Observed by (O):

Reported by (R):

Location:

Students Involved

B = Bully   V = Victim   W = Witnesses

Bullying Behavior

P = Physical   V = Verbal   R = Relational   S = Sexual

Severity/Impact on Victim

1 = Severe   3 = Moderate   5 = Minimal

Intervention:

Comments regarding patterns of bullying episodes:

_____

_____

Comments on intervention and bullying management techniques:

_____

_____

Often, teachers and school leaders will follow up for 8 weeks or longer to assess the intervention impact. Teachers should be aware that the form of bullying may change and that these behaviors may continue. For instance, bullies may shift from physical bullying to verbal or relational forms of bullying. Or, bully supporters may be engaged in similar behaviors until the "dust settles." Therefore, teachers and school leaders may wish to have individual conferences with the bullies, victims, and a sample of witnesses to determine if the behavior has ended. Be aware of inconsistencies in stories.

TALKING WITH FAMILIES AND CAREGIVERS ABOUT BULLYING

Teachers should plan to inform the parents of the bully and the victim as soon as possible. A telephone call to the home the same day that the event occurs is preferable, followed by an appointment at school for the parents or guardians. Parents or guardians of the bully and the victim should not be called to conference together. Results are better when parents are involved early in the bullying situation, before students continue to participate in maladaptive patterns of behavior. Teachers may gather important information at these conferences that will assist them in thinking about prevention and management of bullying behaviors. For instance, teachers may learn that the bullying behavior occurs frequently at home as well as in school or that the bully also has disclosed being a victim of bullying at school. Parents can be wonderful assets in designing a plan of action.

Talking About the Child Who Is a Bully

Family conferences regarding a child who is a bully should be taken very seriously. Plan to spend at least an hour discussing the situation with the parent or guardian. The conference should consist of the following:

- Identifying the behavior the student is demonstrating
- Outlining the policies and procedures regarding bullying behavior in the school and in the classroom, and
- Discussing methods for handling the bullying behaviors both at home and in the classroom

If possible, teachers and school leaders should provide clear evidence (through record keeping) that the student has bullied others. Concisely relay the times, dates, locations, and type of behaviors the student has engaged in with victims. Provide copies of these documents as well as a written copy of the school and/or classroom policy regarding bullying behaviors. As described in Chapter 2, student bullying behaviors often mirror those demonstrated in the home. Therefore, teachers and school leaders should be prepared to manage parents or guardians with similar bullying tendencies. In many cases, parents or guardians will deny that their son or daughter is a bully or will defend bullying as a rite of passage. Clear and consistent record keeping will assist teachers and school leaders in addressing these objections.

Indeed, teachers and school leaders should provide advice for parents and guardians regarding how to address the bullying behavior with their child. Be sure to frame the conference, however, as seeking assistance with the problem behavior and not the student or the victim. Suggestions for parents are provided in Figure 5.6. It is important for school staff to review the suggestions during the conference, in case parents have questions or need additional clarification.

Talking About the Child Who Is a Victim

Parents or guardians should be notified as quickly as possible about the victimization behaviors. Parents of children being victimized should be provided with the following information:

- How the child has been victimized
- The policies and procedures regarding bullying behavior in the school and in the classroom
- Steps that have been taken to secure the safety of the student in the classroom, and
- Methods for handling the bullying behaviors both at home and in the classroom

Figure 5.6   Suggestions for Parent Information: Bullies

- Take the bullying behavior seriously. The behavior will not be tolerated in the classroom or school. Talk with your child about the behavior and its implications. The child may deny, excuse, or minimize the seriousness of the behavior. Let your child know that you will not tolerate the behavior.
- Develop consequences for the bullying behavior. Harsh or hostile punishments may only serve to reinforce the bullying behavior. Ask the child for ideas for appropriate consequences. Consequences are extremely effective if they are consistent across the school and home environments.
- Develop a reinforcement schedule for anti-bullying behaviors demonstrated at home and school. Closely monitor the child's activities at school and frequently request (if they are not automatically provided) reports on your child's behavior. Reinforcement schedules are highly effective if they are consistent across the school and home environments.
- Reduce potential models of bullying behaviors in the home. Reflect on the methods used for conflict resolution in the home, on television, through the computer, and on favorite video games. Use this opportunity to amend viewing habits or make it a teachable moment.
- Seek assistance from professionals if the behavior continues.

Teachers should provide clear evidence (through record keeping) that the student has been victimized. Concisely relay the times, dates, locations, and type of behaviors the student has experienced. Provide copies of these documents as well as a written copy of the school and/or classroom policy regarding bullying behaviors. Be careful not to focus on the bully or to blame the victim, but rather frame the conference as seeking assistance with the problem behavior and not the student or the victim.

Teachers and school leaders also should be prepared to identify the strategies for classroom or schoolwide anti-bullying efforts. If possible, provide parents and guardians with samples of classroom material on assertiveness, empathy, and constructive conflict resolution techniques. Enlist parents' and guardians' assistance with reinforcing these concepts in the home. Specifically, assist parents and guardians with assessing sibling interactions in the home. Encourage the victimized child to try assertion skills with siblings during periods of conflict.

Suggestions for parents of children who are being bullied are provided in Figure 5.7.

Figure 5.7   Suggestions for Parent Information: Victims

- Take the victimization behavior seriously. Assure the child that the behavior will not be tolerated in the classroom or school. Talk with your child about the behavior and its implications. The child may deny, excuse, or minimize the seriousness of the behavior in order to protect the bully and defuse the severity of the situation. Let your child know that you are supportive and empathetic and are ready to help. Your child must know that he or she is being listened to on a consistent basis.

- When your child describes bullying behavior, do not react negatively toward the event or the bully. Aggressing toward the bully's parents or hostile comments regarding supervision at the school will heighten the anxiety and uneasiness that some children will experience when discussing victimization. Never advise children to fight back in victimization situations.

- Develop a reinforcement schedule for prosocial and assertive behaviors demonstrated at home and school. Reinforcement schedules are highly effective if they are consistent across the school and home environments.

- Teach children to express themselves clearly and identify nonverbal ways of conveying assertiveness. Children should practice deep breathing exercises, maintaining eye contact with individuals, keeping hands steady, and assertive body posturing.

- Closely monitor the child's activities at school and frequently request (if they are not automatically provided) reports on your child's behavior. Watch for signs of victimization, such as fear of going to school, ripped or torn clothing, "lost money," or significant changes in a child's behavioral pattern.

- Attempt to provide the child with situations in which he or she can make friends or develop social skills. The goals for the new activities should be to further develop the child's support network and confidence.

- Allow some time for the situation to change. Bully-victim-witness relationships do not occur overnight, and they frequently will not change overnight.

- Reduce potential models of victimization behaviors in the home. Reflect on the methods used for conflict resolution in the home, on television, through the computer, and on favorite video games. Use this opportunity to amend viewing habits or make it a teachable moment.

- Seek assistance from professionals if the behavior continues.

SUMMARY

Careful planning can reduce bullying behavior among students, but it is unlikely that these behaviors can be totally eliminated. Therefore, every school and every teacher must have a strategy for intervening when bullying occurs. The steps outlined in this chapter can be used to stop the bullying, label it as wrong, implement consequences for the behavior, discuss the situation with all parties involved, document it, and discuss ways to prevent it in the future.

It is important to involve both students and parents or guardians in the process and to maintain open lines of communication with all parties involved. Victims can be empowered by learning techniques for responding to bullying and by documenting incidents. Bullies can learn to identify situations in which they will be tempted to bully and to enlist help from adults to stop. Parents can be educated about the signs and causes of bullying and what can be done at home to prevent it. Everyone has an important role to play.

6

Evaluating Anti-Bullying Initiatives

THE IMPORTANCE OF EVALUATION

Evaluating anti-bullying initiatives, whether schoolwide or classroom based, is important for building a strong school environment that is free from bullying behaviors. Teachers and administrators may use evaluation to validate their efforts and may use evaluation data to modify or maintain initiatives. Evaluation tools are also valuable in educating the entire school community on the value of the work and, in turn, may encourage greater support and involvement in implementing effective school programming.

Evaluation of other school safety issues, such as youth violence prevention, has been invaluable and has served as a basis for developing and implementing school-based programs. Evaluation of anti-bullying initiatives, however, is not as prolific as evaluation of youth violence prevention efforts. In fact, anti-bullying efforts in U.S. schools are still relatively new. Therefore, school administrators and teachers do not have as firm a foundation for selecting programming efforts for anti-bullying programs as they do when choosing other school safety initiatives. Unlike evaluating student achievement in an academic content area such as math or the sciences, measurement of student learning through social skill development programming is difficult. This difficulty is due, in part, to

- Lack of previous empirical work in the programming area
- Lack of standardized and consistent goals and objectives in research that does exist, and
- Unreliable and nonstandardized means of measuring student outcomes

Evaluation of programming, regardless of the availability of previous empirical data, is important for anti-bullying initiatives. Results of evaluations may demonstrate the importance of reviewing and modifying the anti-bullying initiatives. The data may also provide important information about why implemented programming initiatives have been effective.

The process of evaluation documents if and how the programming has met the goals and objectives of the anti-bullying plan. For instance, if a structured curriculum program is implemented in all third grade classrooms in a school to combat bullying, an evaluation will interpret if the curriculum met the goal of reducing bullying incidents in the school by third grade students. An evaluation also will provide information on the quality of the delivery of the curriculum by third grade teachers and will support the need for additional or modified programming to address bullying.

Selected Evaluators

Programming initiatives, school or classroom based, may be evaluated by a number of professionals. As discussed in Chapter 3, an important step in implementing a schoolwide approach is to identify who will be responsible for evaluating programming success. In cases of schoolwide programs, evaluation is often conducted with the assistance of an outside evaluator. Evaluators are often quite costly; therefore, the school should consider collaborating with a local college or university. Most universities charge reasonable fees and have the technical assistance capabilities for evaluating community service programs, in addition to a diverse group of graduate students eager to obtain data sets for school requirements. Consulting firms are also available to assist with program evaluation, yet they are often expensive and are not always knowledgeable about the topic they are evaluating. Therefore, providing clear, concise, and measurable goals becomes the sole responsibility of the school personnel. When evaluation consultants have knowledge of the issue they are evaluating, they may assist the anti-bullying committee with developing reasonable and measurable program goals.

Teachers who implement classroom programs should be encouraged to evaluate their own initiatives. Internal evaluators (even the teachers themselves) may be prepared enough to measure classroom-based interventions. Although evaluations are best conducted by objective individuals, valuable information may be collected about classroom programming by teachers. Schools with limited resources, for example, may enlist teachers' support for collecting data so that outside consultant services are limited to statistically analyzing data and developing appropriate recommendations.

Process, Outcome, and Impact Evaluations

Several kinds of evaluations are available to measure anti-bullying programming success: the process evaluation, the outcome evaluation, and the impact evaluation. Schoolwide anti-bullying programs are suited for process, outcome, and impact evaluations, while classroom evaluations traditionally use only outcome and impact evaluations. Classroom evaluations will rarely use process outcomes, because comparison groups are often unavailable (standardization across classrooms isn't possible) and because most classroom programs will involve all students and not merely a few targeted students. A process evaluation may be relevant, although time-consuming, to determine if specific classroom policies or procedures are having an effect on the school's programming goals. Indeed, anti-bullying initiatives may incorporate all three forms of evaluation, which would provide school change agents with the most comprehensive view of programming effectiveness.

Process Evaluations

A process evaluation describes and measures the quality of the implementation of anti-bullying initiatives. This process identifies the level of effectiveness of the delivery of a program. For example, schools may conduct a process evaluation to determine if newly implemented polices and procedures are effective. A school that increases the number of adults during lunchtime or changes the structure of the playground may benefit from a process evaluation.

Process evaluation is also useful to measure how well a program is reaching its intended audience. An initiative may only target first through third grades, and only bullies. The process evaluation will determine if the grades and students are appropriate as sole targets for the school anti-bullying efforts. Although anti-bullying initiatives should include the entire school community and each role in the bully-victim-witness relationship, process evaluation may be useful for schools implementing anti-bullying programming in a step-by-step fashion (for example, curriculum integration, policies, and then programming).

Questions involved in a process evaluation are outlined in Figure 6.1.

Outcome and Impact Evaluations

Outcome and impact evaluations can measure the effect of the programming on student variables. Therefore, while the process evaluation

Figure 6.1   Process Evaluation Questions

- How many students are involved with the program or strategy? Are there similarities or differences among the students? Do they represent the entire student population?
- Are these students the intended audience?
- Are students being exposed to the same type, quality, and amount of programming? What differences occur?
- Is staff adequate in number, level of competence, and motivation to deliver the services?
- Are adequate resources available to support the programming?
- Is administrative, district, and parental support adequate?

measures possible delivery effects, the outcome and impact evaluations identify to what extent delivery affects the program objectives (for example, student variables). An outcome evaluation (see Figure 6.2) studies the immediate effects of an anti-bullying program, and an impact evaluation measures more long-term effects of an intervention. An evaluation might determine whether students demonstrate increased knowledge, improved skills, or better attitudes regarding anti-bullying. It can also identify whether bullying episodes have decreased and prosocial inclusive behaviors have increased. Outcome and impact evaluations will also determine if and how the school climate has changed as a result of the anti-bullying programming.

Outcome and impact evaluations follow traditional patterns of time line implementation and usually incorporate multiple assessments over a programming year. In most cases, outcome evaluations will require, at a minimum, a pretest (prior to implementation) and a posttest (following implementation). Impact evaluations require at least two additional measurements, during implementation and shortly following program implementation. In highly comprehensive impact evaluations, researchers track programming variables several months or years following intervention.

Preprogram and Postprogram Evaluations

Once data is collected, comparisons between baseline (preintervention) data and implementation data can be analyzed. Preprogram and postprogram evaluations are one of the least sophisticated methods but most effective means of evaluating programming success. However, such evaluations cannot determine causality unless evaluators use rigorous statistical sampling procedures. In order to prove that programming caused changes in students' skills, knowledge, or attitudes, intervention classrooms must be randomly assigned to "control" and experimental groups. Control groups must contain students who are representative of the entire

Figure 6.2   Common Outcome Evaluation Questions

- How have new anti-bullying policies and procedures affected the number and type of student code violations in the schools?
- Have students improved their ability to be empathetic, be assertive, and resolve conflict constructively?
- Have classroom management issues declined as a result of classroom anti-bullying initiatives?
- Has a specific anti-bullying curriculum improved classroom climate and/or reduced the incidence of bullying?
- Are students demonstrating an increase in reporting and/or witness intervention?

student population and will not receive any intervention. Comparing control groups and experimental groups using preprogram and postprogram measurement may assist evaluators with the question of whether programming initiatives caused improvements in students' knowledge, skills, and attitudes regarding anti-bullying.

Preprogram and postprogram evaluations are not conducive in all situations, however. If students are not exposed to identical intervention (both content and delivery) for the same period of time, evaluators cannot draw conclusions about the success of the program. Also, if a school implements different programming levels at different times, or multiple violence prevention initiatives (for example, mediation programs plus curriculum), then simple preprogram and postprogram evaluation alone is inappropriate. In this case, a school may determine that students do not demonstrate changes in knowledge, skills, or attitudes. This lack of significant findings may be because anti-bullying curriculum has a significant impact but mediation programming does not (canceling out potential positive effects of curriculum).

Although the true experimental design may be preferable because of the nature of its potential outcomes, it is difficult to conduct within a single school. Students exposed to curriculum in one classroom may use these skills in other classrooms (a control classroom). In addition, if programming is implemented using a schoolwide approach, it is difficult to offer services to some students and not all. Preprogram and postprogram evaluations using a quasi-experimental design are adequate, however, for most schools, identifying program success and demonstrating relationships (not casual links) between student changes prior to versus following program implementation.

The evaluation of anti-bullying initiatives is essential for building safer school environments. The evaluation process will provide evidence that initiatives are working, need modifications, or need to be replaced with alternative programming. The evaluation process also validates the importance of the work conducted in the classroom and school setting.

EVALUATION METHODS

Evaluation Through Observation

The easiest method for evaluating anti-bullying efforts is through observations. Observations may be *unstructured,* as when an observer selects a time and location in which bullying is likely to occur (for example, playground, lunchroom, restroom), or *structured,* when an observer selects a focal student or students to study. Researchers have found observation an important tool for understanding the process of peer victimization such as social status issues, social isolation, and social withdrawal (Kinney, 1993; Merton, 1996).

Record keeping that includes observation is an excellent tool for identifying changes in student behavior prior to and following program implementation. Evaluators may observe a random sample of students, fewer than the entire class (or school), or may focus on a few students to determine change over time. Data collection is most useful if clearly defined categories and types of behaviors are outlined. For example, evaluators may define bullying as physical aggression that includes hitting, shoving, pushing, and kicking but not verbal aggression. Observers would then record the frequency, magnitude, and duration of the defined behavior.

The least sophisticated method for evaluating anti-bullying efforts, observation may not measure the true prevalence and magnitude of bullying behavior, as bullying is often covert (Colvin, Tobin, Beard, Hagan, & Sprague, 1998; Olweus, 1993). Pelligrini (1998) suggests the use of student observational methods or diaries in which youth record their own and others' behavior on standardized forms prepared for them. Diaries are particularly useful in middle school, allowing students to inform the evaluator about bullying behavior occurring in their complex social networks.

Interviews and Focus Groups

Interviews and focus groups are alternative methods for evaluating the effects of anti-bullying initiatives. Glover, Gough, Johnson, and Cartwright (2000) cited that students have an opportunity in interviews to speak about issues regarding bullying that may not be typically addressed in other evaluation methods. An effective method for gathering data, interviews and focus groups should be conducted by objective persons with some skill to probe participants (that is, students and/or teachers). In many cases, a school psychologist or social worker (district- or school building-level) would best serve to conduct interview sessions.

Interviews typically occur one on one, while focus groups generally convene with one interviewer, a response recorder, and no more than ten students. Effective focus groups should take no longer than 2 hours to conduct and therefore are time efficient, while an individual interview

Figure 6.3   Sample Interview and Focus Group Questions

- Do you feel safe in your classroom/school?
- What makes you feel unsafe?
- Tell me about students being bullied in the classroom/school.
- Tell me about the students who are bullying other students in the classroom/school?
- Describe how the anti-bullying initiative (fill in specific type) is helping make the classroom/ school safe for students.
- What changes in the classroom/school have you seen since the anti-bullying initiative (fill in specific type) has been implemented?
- What are some actions that principals, teachers, and parents or guardians could take to prevent bullying behavior in the classroom/school?

process is quite time-consuming. Student responses in interviews and focus groups can be transcribed and coded to examine multiple aspects of bullying, increasing the time commitment for this method. Sample interview and focus group questions are provided in Figure 6.3.

Indeed, a challenge to using interviews and focus groups to evaluate anti-bullying efforts is the reliability of the data collection. Interviews and focus groups can be subjective and biased because of preconceptions or viewpoints of the interviewers. As well, when interviews and focus groups are conducted by teachers and/or school administrators, students may be more concerned about revealing sensitive information and may be less willing to reveal information about the effectiveness of intervention strategies.

The Selman model (1980), described in Chapter 4, provides a mechanism for measuring students' changes in skills related to constructive conflict resolution and perspective taking. It does not, however, measure performance of these skills. One may use the Selman model through an interview method as a means of (1) assessing students' sociocognitive interpersonal negotiation strategy and (2) understanding changes over time following anti-bullying program implementation.

Students should be asked to review a hypothetical situation and answer several open-ended questions regarding the situation. A sample evaluation form is presented in Figure 6.4.

The hypothetical situation presented in Figure 6.4 outlines a potential problem involving two or more characters. The goal of using this model is to determine students' level of functioning on a 0–3 scale based on the adapted Selman (1980) model. Evaluators should attempt to score each question separately, depending on the level of sophistication of the response with regard to perspective taking. For example, in answer to the first question, a student may respond that Sara likes the new student more than Laura. This is a significantly lower level response (0–1) than a

Figure 6.4   Sample Evaluation Form

Hypothetical Situation

Sara (James) is best friends with Laura (Mark). A new student comes to the school and Sara (James) spends more time with the new student than with Laura (Mark).

Open-Ended Questions

1. What is the problem?
2. How does Laura (Mark) feel?
3. How does Sara (James) feel?
4. What are some ways to solve the problem?
5. What is the best way to solve the problem?

---

response like, "Sara is spending more time with a new student and Laura is probably feeling a little hurt and left out." Similar scores may be identified with regards to questions 4 and 5 regarding solutions. Students may answer question 5 as "Mark should just dump James as a friend" (a lower level of functioning), or "Mark and James might find a way to spend time together either alone or with the new student" (a higher, more collaborative method).

Teachers may use the Selman model as a fast yet effective method for measuring changes in sociocognitive ability following interventions such as anti-bullying programs. One method is to identify students' level of function prior to programming and to compare this with the developmentally appropriate responses for students that age. For instance, 200 middle schools are scheduled to participate in anti-bullying programming. The evaluation determines that 25 percent of all participating students respond at a 0–1 level, substantially lower than developmentally expected. Seventy-five percent of students demonstrate higher-level responses. Following program implementation, evaluators present another, similar hypothetical situation. This time, only 10 percent of students respond at a 0–1 level, and 90 percent respond in developmentally appropriate ways. In this case, the Selman model has quickly documented the success of the programming.

In addition to evaluating overall changes in student responses, those who have implemented classroom-based programs may wish to evaluate individual changes. To do this, evaluators must determine each student's level both prior to and following implementation. This will be particularly useful in determining if differences in effects occurred depending on the students' roles in the bully-victim-witness relationship.

Surveys and Questionnaires

School administrators and teachers may use surveys as a method to evaluate students' behaviors in the classroom, on the playground, and in the lunchroom. Two of the best surveys for assessing anti-bullying initiatives are the School Social Behavior Scales (SSBS) and the Achenbach Teacher Report Form (TRF) (Achenbach, 1994). Parents can complete the Achenbach Child Behavior Checklist (CBCL) (Achenbach, 1994) to determine changes in student behavior at home. The Olweus Bully/Victim Questionnaire (OBVQ) (Olweus, 1983) is an inventory that was designed to assess bully and victim problems in schools. The OBVQ identifies students' perceptions of the extent of bullying, location where bullying takes place, reporting behaviors, and intervention success. Crick and Grotpeter (1995) developed the Social Experience Questionnaire (SEQ) to measure relational aggression apart from the other kinds of bullying. In this self-report, students identify how often they have experienced certain victimization behaviors.

Attitudinal change in students following anti-bullying initiatives is often difficult to create and to measure, particularly because students are not likely to respond truthfully to socially undesirable questions regarding bullying and victimization behaviors. Teachers should consider using the Normative Orientation to Beliefs about Aggression Scale (NOBAGS) for students in elementary and middle school. The 20-item scale, developed by Huesmann, Guerra, and Zelli (1994), measures a student's perception on the desirability of aggressive responses in a hypothetical situation.

Finally, teachers may wish to consider using surveys as a method for measuring the classroom climate prior to and following program implementation. Surveys similar to the assessment survey provided in Chapter 3, Figure 3.2, may also be used to identify student perceptions of classroom and school safety. The Safe and Responsive Schools Survey (SSRS) is an excellent tool to determine changes in the classroom and/or school climate following anti-bullying initiatives. The SSRS is available for use by school leaders to measure students,' teachers,' and parents' and guardians' perceptions of school safety.

SUMMARY

Careful evaluation of anti-bullying initiatives is essential. Administrators must determine the effectiveness of the various components of their programming so that they may continue with successful techniques and modify those that are not working as well. Documenting successful anti-bullying initiatives can also lead to greater community support for the programs and, in some cases, funding.

Evaluating programming can be costly, especially if schools use outside consulting firms. Often, a better alternative is to partner with a local college or university that may have the necessary resources to conduct the evaluation at a much lower cost. For classroom-based initiatives, school staff may be able to conduct an adequate evaluation without outside assistance.

Evaluators can use process, outcome, or impact evaluations—or some combination of the three—to form opinions about program effectiveness. Process evaluations will measure factors such as the intended audience of the programming and the resources and staff available to implement it. Outcome and impact evaluations measure the immediate and long-term effects of programming on students. Many educators have found the Selman model (1980) especially helpful in measuring the success of anti-bullying education. Through interviews, observation, and/or surveys, teachers and administrators should be able to gather the necessary data to thoroughly evaluate, and ultimately strengthen, their anti-bullying initiatives.

7

Legislation Regarding Bullying Behavior

Incidents of youth violence in schools across America have prompted educators and public officials to create and implement policies regarding bullying. These new policies are a much-needed attempt to respond to physical and verbal bullying; they often recognize relational forms of bullying behaviors as well. The hope is that that the new legislation will prevent, or at least reduce, school violence in the future and protect victims from negative social and academic outcomes.

Legislation requiring schools to act upon bullying is not without controversy, however. Opponents of the legislative measures often argue that to mandate school policy through legislative means is excessive and that individual schools do not have the means to police behavior. Much of the legislation proposed by states currently does not provide for funding to support its implementation. Therefore, schools bear the financial responsibility for supporting initiatives consistent with legislative trends. Policy requiring greater surveillance of school buildings, additional personnel to supervise lunchrooms or playgrounds, or additional school counselors can be expensive and not immediately possible for schools to implement. School administrators and faculty view the legislative initiatives as increasing their already burdened financial resources. In addition, regulatory policies often do not include a measure for evaluating school compliance, either for punitive purposes or to reward schools that do comply with the regulations. The lack of a good system for holding schools accountable compromises the effectiveness of these important initiatives.

In addition, some opponents have viewed the legislative trends as opposing the First Amendment's guarantee of freedom of speech. These opponents state that most schools have suitable policies on appropriate speech at school that should cover verbal bullying behavior. They contend that anti-bullying legislation is merely being used to protect youth with alternative sexual orientations, that it is creating pro-homosexual and not anti-bullying legislation.

Other opponents of anti-bullying legislation question its effectiveness. Such legislation is so new that little is known about its effectiveness in easing bullying behaviors in schools. Some well-known public health advocates concerned with the issue of violence, such as Prothrow-Stith (as cited in Zehr, 2001), believe that the anti-bullying legislation trend holds little promise because it tends to distract individuals from developing preventive methods. Much of the current legislation regarding school bullying involves policies implemented after bullying occurs. Legislative trends do not outline the necessary preventive steps to deal proactively with anti-bullying initiatives, nor do they fully fund such initiatives. Legislative trends may be more promising if prescriptive in nature as opposed to punitive.

Support for anti-bullying legislation also is often questioned because it closely mirrors another controversial issue: character education. Critics of character education view any legislative initiatives dealing with character as potentially usurping the role of parents in teaching their children. Critics feel parents should teach children how to treat other people respectfully and value others. As with character education, critics of anti-bullying legislation believe that it shouldn't be a component of schools' programming but rather should be taught in the home.

Indeed, uniform policies mandated by legislation are often challenged in courts. For example, zero tolerance laws are often challenged, with parents and students arguing that expulsions without regard to circumstances are too harsh. Students also suggest that uniform disciplinary actions do not afford teachers the discretion to respond to specific classroom situations. State law should provide guidance and support for school officials where choices are unclear.

Another controversy surrounds the use of student profiling policies, in which school staff study traits that may be associated with a tendency toward violence. For instance, in instituting student profiling legislation, Maine and New Mexico have taken steps to make sure that educators in their states are trained to spot potential problems and intervene when needed. Although widely used to prevent school violence, these new profiling policies are still being debated in many school districts. Among the concerns raised is the possibility that the profiling policies may violate students' rights, exposing school districts to potential lawsuits as a result of bias-based discrimination. A related issue with student profiling is whether empirical evidence exists to support the effectiveness of this technique.

Despite opposition, the rising recognition of bullying as a serious public health concern has resulted in a significant amount of legislative, policy, and programmatic activity in recent years.

LEGAL IMPLICATIONS FOR SCHOOLS

Schools that cannot prove they are taking bullying behavior seriously may expose themselves to legal action if the bullying results in injury to youth in the school. It may not be enough for schools and legislators to say that they have anti-bullying policies and programming in place. Rather, if a school administrator or school faculty member knows that bullying is occurring, but fails to take an appropriate or effective action, that individual could be found guilty of negligence, and victims could seek compensatory damages for psychological harm. For instance, in Great Britain, parents of a child brought suit against the school for not protecting their child in a bullying situation. Administrators of an all-boys school in London, England, were unable to expel a bully; therefore, the victim's mother enrolled her son in another school. The mother stated that administration was unable to provide the necessary reassurances to allow the victim to return to the school. In another incident, a school in Queens, New York City, faced an investigation claiming that children were bullied on numerous occasions and that the principal did not respond adequately to protect children from bullying behavior.

Intervening may also pose problems for school staff if the intervention is not done appropriately. In another case, the *Chicago Sun-Times* ("Bullying is rampant," 2001) reported a teacher taking a stand against bullying and being reprimanded because of his unusual strategies to rid the school of bullies. The teacher's methods included calling the boys "gangbangers" and following them in his car as they walked from school. Clearly, school staff face a challenge, as both their actions or their failure to act may later be called into question.

Statewide Legislation

State laws have been the primary mechanism for recent anti-bullying initiatives, as states have a greater potential to influence the policies and practices of local school districts. Since 2001, fifteen states have passed laws addressing bullying among schoolchildren, and many other states are considering such legislation.

Sometimes states develop legislation that is uniform statewide. In other cases, they may allow for some flexibility that enables individual school districts to determine policies and procedures appropriate to meet the needs of their student populations. Arkansas, Kentucky, and Tennessee have enacted laws mandating statewide disciplinary codes. Other states, such as Alabama, Colorado, Georgia, New York, and Vermont, either require or allow school districts or state education boards to implement their own approaches.

Indeed, the effectiveness of state legislation in protecting students from bullying has yet to be determined. Limber (2002) cited that the effectiveness of legislation will depend largely on how closely laws infuse social science research on bullying. Effective legislation must define bullying, the nature and seriousness of bullying, and how school policies and procedures must address bullying.

Defining Bullying

State laws must specifically define the behaviors associated with bullying so as to avoid ambiguity for school administrators and state education departments. However, many states have not developed laws that contain specific and accurate definitions of bullying behaviors, as identified by bullying researchers. Georgia's legislation cites a narrow definition of bullying, emphasizing the physical act of bullying and not verbal or relational behaviors. Colorado law addresses a more expansive definition, including both verbal and physical bullying, but does not include more indirect forms of bullying. Legislators in Louisiana, Oklahoma, and Washington liken bullying to harassment and intimidation, often leading to inaccurate connections between the nature of bullying and harassment behaviors. New Jersey also addresses bullying and harassment behaviors in legislation, but notes that districts may choose to consider acts of bullying that are not covered by the statute.

Limiting Teacher Liability

Teachers' rights are also an issue. Some states are also concerned about the legal liability teachers now face as the result of anti-bullying legislation. Teacher protection and limits on liability for teachers are also quite common, with more than 20 states actively securing limits on teacher liability. Teachers in Alaska, Colorado, and Florida passed laws exempting school staff from liability when acting within the scope of their employment. For instance, any person in Colorado carrying out a teacher's authority to suspend or expel a student, in good faith, has civil and criminal immunity. These laws protect teachers and other school officials from legal challenges to their behavior, short of extreme departures from school policy.

Other states clearly specify the limits of exemption from reporting. In South Carolina, school administrators and school districts that fail to report school-related crimes are liable for attorney's fees as well as any costs from legal actions requiring the school to make such reports. New York offers civil immunity for school employees who had reasonable cause to suspect and report violent acts. Basic tort law applies, and school officials may be responsible for harm caused when they do something, or fail to do something, connected to a violent act. Students have sued educators and schools for failing to protect them from hazing, hate crimes, bullying, or other violent behaviors.

Staff Training

Staff training on the nature and outcomes of bullying behaviors is a critical component of state legislation. California, Connecticut, and Maine have developed programs to train teachers in conflict management, effective classroom discipline, or warning signs of violent behavior. Unfortunately, few states currently address provisions for employee training specifically on bullying prevention. Legislation in New Hampshire and West Virginia encourage but do not mandate staff training, emphasizing that schools should be providing training on the harassment, intimidation, or bullying policy if funds are available for such purposes. Washington's legislation not only requires school districts to provide staff training on harassment, intimidation, and bullying prevention policy, but mandates the maintenance of a Web site through the office of the superintendent of public instruction that contains model policies, practices, and recommended training materials.

Bullying Prevention Policies, Strategies, and Programs

State laws vary greatly as to how they address bullying prevention policies, strategies, and programs. A common element in many state laws is a requirement that administrators develop a policy prohibiting bullying. States such as Georgia, Illinois, Louisiana, New York, New Hampshire, and Washington require districts to have anti-bullying policies and place responsibility for their development on school board members. Other states (for example, California, Vermont) require or recommend that policies be developed by staff at each school building as part of the school's safety plan. Districtwide policies standardize practices across schools in the district, reducing ambiguity among students, staff, and parents. Building-based policies often encourage input from key stakeholders (for example, parents, staff, students). In 2001, Colorado began to require school districts to develop policies regarding bullying prevention and education, but mandates the school principal to report annually on the implementation of the policies, strategies, and programs.

School personnel that require technical assistance in the development of bullying prevention policies are assisted in states such as Colorado, New Hampshire, New Jersey, and Washington with model policies or published technical advisories. In 2002, the New Jersey Department of Education issued one of the most comprehensive guides to policy development, emphasizing potential pitfalls and mechanisms to overcome struggles associated with anti-bullying policy implementation.

Mechanisms for Addressing Bullies and Protecting Victims

State laws rarely address both disciplinary procedures for bullies and the protection of victims. Rather, state law more frequently address disciplinary action for students who bully their peers. New Jersey and West Virginia mandate that school districts include consequences and remedial action for perpetrators in their bullying policies, although the law does not stipulate specific actions. Georgia law mandates that students (Grades 6–12) who have committed the offense of bullying for the third time in a school year must be transferred to another school. According to Limber (2002) legislating student exclusion as a means of preventing bullying may undermine bullying prevention efforts.

Indeed, only one state specifically addresses the protection of victims of bullying behavior. West Virginia requires each county board of education to establish policies that protect victims from additional harassment from school bullies.

LEGISLATIVE TRENDS

California. School districts must have a comprehensive school safety plan that must include an anti-discrimination and harassment policy and procedures for reporting hate crimes specifically. The Legislature also required the state Department of Education to develop model policies on the prevention of bullying and conflict resolution.

Colorado. Perhaps the most comprehensive legislative act occurred in Colorado in May 2001. The General Assembly declared that bullying disrupts a school's ability to educate students and threatens public safety by creating an atmosphere in which such behavior has the potential for violence. The bill requires that all school safety plans include a policy that creates an environment free from bullying. Specific policies concerning bullying prevention and education are required as part of this policy. Bullying is defined by the legislation as any written or verbal expression or physical act or gesture or a pattern that is intended to cause distress for one or more students in the school, on school grounds, in school vehicles, at any designated school bus stop, or at school activities or sanctioned events.

As a result of this legislation, schools throughout Colorado, such as in Jefferson County Public Schools, are implementing the SERA Learning behavioral skills programs, Skills for Managing Anger, and the Program for Young Negotiators. Legislation also requires schools to provide yearly progress reports to the state.

Connecticut. In 2001, the Connecticut legislature passed House Bill 7502, an act concerning expenditures for the programs and services of the Department of Education. The act requires the Department of Education to establish, within available appropriations, a competitive safe learning grant program to assist schools with a number of school safety programs, including those designed to eliminate bullying behaviors among students. This bill was extremely controversial in the state, as it was spearheaded by members of the Parent Teacher Association of Connecticut yet neglected to require schools to include parents in assisting schools with the development and implementation of the safe school programming. In May 2002, specific school bullying legislation, with steps to prevent bullying behavior, passed the House.

Georgia. In July 1999, the House of Representatives enacted legislation stating that codes for elementary and secondary education must include bullying behavior. Georgia has identified education regarding bullying behaviors as a part of character education. Therefore, the State Board of Education of Georgia addresses methods of discouraging bullying behaviors as a component of their comprehensive character education program. The legislation also requires that bullying be clearly defined, that local boards of education adopt policies that prohibit bullying behaviors for students in Grades 6–12, and that students guilty of engaging in bullying behavior three or more times be assigned to alternative schools. The legislation also provides for notification of students and parents regarding anti-bullying policies.

Illinois. In House Bill 646, the state of Illinois, in 2001, passed anti-bullying legislation mandating that the school board, in consultation with the parent-teacher advisory committee and other community-based organizations, include within their discipline policy students who demonstrate bullying behaviors. The legislation also requires procedures for notifying parents or guardians of bullying behaviors and procedures for early intervention based on community-based and district resources available.

Michigan. Michigan is currently considering more comprehensive legislative measures aimed at bullying, yet hesitates as it recently passed strong laws regarding school violence. The state Board of Education strongly recommends that schools adopt anti-bullying policies and has assisted with this effort by revising the student code of conduct. In addition, anti-bullying lessons have become infused into the Michigan standardized curriculum model, called the "Michigan Model."

New Hampshire. New Hampshire's law allows local school boards to create anti-bullying policies and provides disciplinary procedures for students who subject others to "insults, taunts, or challenges, whether verbal or physical in nature." The legislation also requires that bullying behavior be reported, and if such behavior is reported, the school employee is immune from action that may arise from the failure to remedy the reported incident. No specific curriculum, textbook, or presentation is required. The law recommends that anti-bullying programs be implemented, but does not mandate that schools implement them. School districts must notify parents or legal guardians of the district's policies on bullying and require that a report of any bullying incidents be made by telephone and by a written report sent by mail to the parent or legal guardian of the students involved.

New Jersey. Each school district is required to develop a policy against harassment, intimidation, and bullying. Each district's policy must contain certain elements including definitions for acceptable and unacceptable behavior, consequences, and appropriate remediation procedures for reporting and investigating violations. The bill also requires the code to be incorporated into school employee training programs. As in West Virginia law, New Jersey law provides immunity from a cause of action for damages arising from the reporting of an incident to individuals who make that report in good faith and in compliance with established procedures.

Oklahoma. The School Bullying Prevention Act orders school districts to devise specific plans to reduce violence and create a safer learning environment. Safe School Committees (SSCs) were established by law to issue recommendations about school safety to each school principal. Each SSC is required to pay special attention to bullying, physical and verbal aggression, and sexual harassment.

Oregon. In June 2001, the Oregon House and Senate approved anti-bullying legislation sponsored by Representative Richard Devlin. This bill directs the superintendent of public instruction to develop a model policy prohibiting harassment, intimidation, or bullying on school grounds, at school activities, on school vehicles, or at school bus stops. Anonymous reporting is allowed, yet it cannot be used as the sole basis for determining disciplinary action. The bill allows immunity for teaching staff who promptly report the bullying behavior.

Tennessee. Requires each Local Educational Agency (LEA) to adopt a policy that prohibits harassment, intimidation, or bullying. Legislation encourages school employees, volunteers, and students to report incidents of harassment, intimidation, or bullying to the appropriate school authorities, and provides school personnel who report harassment, intimidation, or bullying with immunity against any suit.

Vermont. Legislation directs schools to include bullying in their policies for responding to misconduct on and off school grounds, and directs the commissioner of education to update model policies on student discipline to include a definition of bullying, a process for reporting acts of bullying, and responses to bullying.

Virginia. Legislation directs the Board of Education to include bullying in its standards for school board policies on student conduct and requires school boards to include (1) instruction on the inappropriateness of bullying in their character education programs, and (2) bullying provisions in their student conduct codes. Law requires school principals to report certain violent acts, stalking, and other conduct to parents of the minor student who is the target of the conduct.

Washington State. Washington legislature vested sole authority for policy development with the Office of the Superintendent of Public Instruction (OSPI). School districts were required to adopt the OSPI's model policy on harassment, intimidation, and bullying or amend an existing policy to be in compliance. In addition to the anti-bullying policy that all schools were required to adopt, the Washington superintendent of public instruction disseminated teacher training materials and conducted workshops and other school staff development activities to ensure uniform, statewide education about the policy and responsibilities of school staff in enforcement. In addition, the Legislature appropriated $500,000 to fund bullying prevention programs.

West Virginia. Each county school board is required to develop and adopt a policy to prohibit harassment, intimidation, or bullying through a process that involves parents, school personnel, students, and community members. West Virginia law provides immunity from a cause of action for damages arising from the reporting of an incident to individuals who make that report in good faith. Each school district must train teachers and educate students on the anti-bullying and harassment policy if state and/or federal funds are appropriated to do so.

SUMMARY

A great deal of energy has gone into the creation of new legislation designed to prevent bullying incidents in our schools. These initiatives are so new that empirical data regarding their effectiveness is limited. Some programs, including zero tolerance policies and student profiling, are controversial. Schools may question the effectiveness of the programs or feel they lack the staff or funds to properly implement them. Others wonder if the new initiatives are an overreaction to the problem, or even a violation of students' rights.

Nonetheless, the trend seems to be toward mandating anti-bullying education. Schools, and in some cases individual staff members, face the possibility of legal action if they fail to intervene in a bullying situation and a student is harmed as a result. Clearly, the days of ignoring the school bully are finally over.

References

Achenbach, T. (1994). Child behavior checklist and related instruments. In M. Maruishish (Ed.), *The use of psychological testing for treatment planning and outcome assessment* (pp. 525–527). Hillsdale, NJ: Lawrence Erlbaum.

Atlas, R., & Pepler, D. (1998). Observations of bullying in the classroom. *Journal of Educational Research, 92,* 86–99.

Azmitia, M., & Hesser, J. (1993). Why siblings are important agents of cognitive development: A comparison of siblings and peers. *Child Development, 64,* 430–444.

Bandura, A. (1973). *Aggression: A social learning analysis.* Englewood Cliffs, NJ: Prentice Hall.

Barth, J., Dane, H., Dunlap, S., Lochman, J., & Wells, K. (2001, April). *Classroom and school environment influences on aggression, peer acceptance, and academic focus.* Paper presented at the biennial meeting of the Society of Research in Child Development, Minneapolis, MN.

Barton, E. (2000). *Leadership strategies for safe schools.* Arlington Heights, IL: SkyLight Training and Publishing.

Batsche, G. (1997). Bullying. In G. C. Bear, K. M. Minke, & A. Thomas (Eds.), *Children's needs II: Development, problems, and alternatives* (pp. 171–179). Bethesda, MD: National Association of School Psychologists.

Bender, D., & Losel, F. (1997). Protective and risk effects of peer relations and social support on antisocial behavior in adolescents from multi-problem milieus. *Journal of Adolescence, 20,* 661–678.

Berenstain, S., & Berenstain, J. (1995). *The Berenstain bears and too much teasing.* New York: Random House.

Berthold, K., & Hover, J. (2000). Correlates of bullying and victimization among intermediate students in the midwestern USA. *School Psychology International, 21*(1), 65–78.

Besag, V. (1989). *Bullies and victims in schools: A guide to understanding and management.* Milton Keynes, UK: Open University Press.

Besag, V. (1991). The playground. In M. Elliott (Ed.), *Bullying: A practical guide to coping for schools* (pp. 8–14). Harlow, UK: Longman.

Bjorkqvist, K., Ekman, K., & Lagerspetz, K. (1982). Bullies and victims: Their ego picture, ideal ego picture, and normative ego picture. *Scandinavia Journal of Psychology, 23,* 307–313.

Bjorkqvist, K., Lagerspetz, K., & Kaukianinen, A. (1992). Do girls manipulate and boys fight? Developmental trends in regard to direct and indirect aggression. *Aggressive Behavior, 18,* 117–127.

Bullying is rampant in America's schools. (2001, April 25). *Chicago Sun-Times.*

Carney, J. V. (2000). Bullied to death: Perceptions of peer abuse and suicidal behavior during adolescence. *School Psychology International, 21,* 213–223.

Charach, M., Pepler, D., & Ziegler, R. (1995). Bullying at school: A Canadian perspective. *Education Canada, 35,* 12–18.

Colvin, G., Tobin, R., Beard, K., Hagan, S., & Sprague, J. (1998). The school bully: Assessing the problem, developing interventions, and future research directions. *Journal of Behavioral Education, 8,* 293–319.

Committee for Children. (1998). *Steps to Respect: A bullying prevention program.* Seattle, WA: Author.

Compas, B., Slavin, L., Wagner, B., & Vannatta, K. (1986). Relationship of life events and social support with psychological dysfunction among adolescents. *Journal of Youth Adolescence, 15,* 205–221.

Cowie, H. (1998). Perspectives of teachers and pupils on the experience of peer support against bullying. *Educational Research and Evaluation, 4,* 108–125.

Craig, E., Henderson, K., & Murphy, J. (2000). Prospective teachers' attitudes toward bullying and victimization. *School Psychology International, 21,* 5–21.

Craig, W., & Pepler, D. (1997). Observations of bullying and victimization in the school yard. *Canadian Journal of School Psychology, 13*(2), 41–60.

Crick, N., Casas, J., & Ku, H. (1999). Physical and relational peer victimization in preschool. *Developmental Psychology, 33,* 579–588.

Crick, N., & Grotpeter, J. (1995). Relational aggression, gender, and social-psychological adjustment. *Child Development, 66,* 710–722.

Crick, N., & Grotpeter, J. (1996). Children's treatment by peers: Victims of relational and overt aggression. *Development and Psychopathology, 8,* 367–380.

Cummings, E., Vogel, D., Cummings, J., & El-Sheikh, M. (1989). Children's responses to different forms of anger between adults. *Child Development, 60,* 1392–1404.

Deutsch, M. (1993). Educating for a peaceful world. *American Psychologist, 48,* 510–517.

DeVoe, J., & Kaffenberger, S. (2005). *Student reports of bullying: Results from the 2001 school crime supplement to the National Crime Victimization Survey* (NCES 205-310). U.S. Department of Education Statistics. Washington, DC: U.S. Government Printing Office.

Doll, B., Siemers, E., Nickolite, M., & Song, S. (2003, April). *Using ClassMaps Consultation to make classrooms healthy places to learn.* Paper presented at the annual meeting of National Association of School Psychologists, Toronto, Ontario, Canada.

Ennett, S., & Bauman, K. (1996). Adolescent social networks: School, demographic and longitudinal considerations. *Journal of Adolescent Research, 11,* 194–245.

Eron, L. D., Huesmann, R., Dubow, E., Romanoff, R., & Yarmel, P. (1987). Childhood aggression and its correlates over 22 years. In D. H. Crowell, I. Evans, & C. O'Donnell (Eds.), *Childhood aggression and violence: Sources of influence, prevention, and control.* New York: Plenum.

Espelage, D., & Asidao, C. (2001). Interviews with middle school students: Bullying, victimization, and contextual variables. *Journal of Emotional Abuse, 2,* 49–62.

Espelage, D., & Holt, M. (2001). Interviews with middle school students: Bullying, victimization, and contextual variables. *Journal of Emotional Abuse, 2*, 123–142.

Farrington, D. (1991). Childhood aggression and adult violence: Early precursors and later-life outcomes. In D. Pepler & K. Rubin (Eds.), *The development and treatment of childhood aggression* (pp. 5–29). Hillsdale, NJ: Erlbaum.

Frey, C., & Rothlisberger, C. (1996). Social support in healthy adolescents. *Journal of Youth and Adolescence, 25*, 17–31.

Froschl, M., Sprung, B., & Mullin-Rindler, N. (1998). *Quit It! A teacher's guide on teasing and bullying for use with students in grades K–3.* Wellesley, MA: Wellesley Centers for Women.

Furman, W., & Buhrmester, D. (1985). Children's perceptions of personal relationships in their social networks. *Developmental Psychology, 21*, 1016–1024.

Galen, B., & Underwood, J. (1997). A developmental investigation of social aggression among children. *Developmental Psychology, 33*, 589–600.

Garrity, C., Jens, K., Porter, W., et al. (2000). *Bully proofing your school: A comprehensive approach for elementary schools.* Longmont, CO: Sopris West.

Glover, D., Gough, G., Johnson, M., & Cartwright, N. (2000). Bullying in 25 secondary schools: Incidence, impact, and intervention. *Educational Research, 42*, 141–156.

Golding, W. (1954). *Lord of the flies.* New York: Berkley Publishing Group.

Gordon, T. (1970). *Parent effectiveness training.* New York: Peter H. Wyden.

Hanish, L., & Guerra, N. (2000). The roles of ethnicity and school context in predicting children's victimization by peers. *American Journal of Community Psychology, 28*, 201–223.

Hazler, J., Carney, J., Green, S., Powell, R., & Jolly, L. (1997). Areas of expert agreement on identification of school bullies and victims. *School Psychology International, 18*, 5–14.

Higgins, C. (1994). Improving the school ground environment: An anti-bullying intervention. In P. K. Smith & S. Shard (Eds.), *School bullying: Insights and perspective.* London: Routledge.

Hoover, J., Oliver, R., & Thomson, K. (1993). Perceived victimization by school bullies: New research and future direction. *Journal of Humanistic Education and Development, 32*, 76–84.

Howes, P., & Markman, H. J. (1989). Marital quality and child functioning: A longitudinal investigation. *Child Development, 60*, 1044–1051.

Huesmann, L. R., Guerra, N., & Zelli, A. (1994). *Normative orientation to beliefs about aggression scale (NOBAGS).* Unpublished. Ann Arbor, MI: University of Michigan Research Center for Group Dynamics, Institute for Social Research.

Huttunen, A., Salmivalli, C., & Lagerspetz, K. (1996). Friendship networks and bullying in schools. *Annals of the New York Academy of Sciences, 794*, 355–359.

Jeffrey, L., Miller, D., & Linn, M. (2001). Middle school bullying as a context for the development of passive observers to the victimization of others. *Journal of Emotional Abuse, 2*, 143–156.

Johnson, D., & Johnson, R. (1995a). *Teaching students to be peacemakers.* Minneapolis: Burgess.

Johnson, D., & Johnson, R. (1995b). Why violence prevention programs don't work, and what does. *Leadership Education, 52*, 63–68.

Kindersley, B., & Kindersley, A. (1997). *Children just like me.* New York: DK Publishing.

Kinney, D. (1993). From nerds to normals: The recovery of identity among adolescents from middle school to high school. *Sociology of Education, 66*, 21–40.

Kipnis, A. (1999). *Angry young men: How parents, teachers, and counselors can help "bad boys" become good men.* San Francisco: Jossey-Bass.

Limber, S. (2002). Addressing youth bullying behaviors. *Proceedings of the Educational Forum on Adolescent Health: Youth Bullying.* Chicago: American Medical Association.

Llewellyn, A. (2000). Perceptions of mainstreaming: A systems approach. *Developmental Medicine and Child Neurology, 42*, 106–115.

Maccoby, E., & Martin, J. (1983). Socialization in the context of family. In A. J. Sameroff, M. Lewis, & S. Miller (Eds.), *Handbook of developmental psychopathology* (pp. 75–91). New York: Plenum.

Malecki, C., & Demaray, M. (2002). Measuring perceived social support: Development of the Child and Adolescent Social Support Scale. *Psychology in the Schools, 39*, 1–18.

Malecki, C., & Demaray, M. (2003). What type of support do they need? Investigating student adjustment as related to emotional, informational, appraisal, and instrumental support. *School Psychology Quarterly, 18*, 231–252.

Mellor, A. (1991). Helping victims. In M. Elliott (Ed.), *Bullying: A practical guide to coping in schools.* UK: Pearson Education.

Merton, D. (1996). Visibility and vulnerability: Responses to rejection by non-aggressive junior high school boys. *Journal of Early Adolescence, 16*, 5–26.

Nansel, T., Overpeck, M., et al. (2001). Bullying behaviors among U.S. youth: Prevalence and association with psychosocial adjustment. *Journal of the American Medical Association, 285*(16), 2094–2100.

National Center for Education Statistics. (1995). *Student victimization at school* (NCES 95-204). Washington, DC: U.S. Department of Education.

Nelson, D., & Crick, N. (2001). Parental psychological control: Implications for childhood physical and relational aggression. In B. Barber (Ed.), *Intrusive parenting: How psychological control affects children and adolescents* (pp. 161–189). Washington, DC: American Psychological Association.

Olweus, D. (1978). *Aggression in the schools: Bullies and whipping boys.* Washington, DC: Hemisphere (Wiley).

Olweus, D. (1980). Familial and temperamental determinants of aggressive behavior in adolescent boys: A causal analysis. *Developmental Psychology, 16*, 644–660.

Olweus, D. (1983). *Bully/Victim Questionnaire.* Unpublished manuscript, University of Bergen, Norway.

Olweus, D. (1991). Bully/victim problems among schoolchildren: Basic facts and effects of a school-based intervention program. In D. Pepeler & K. Rubin, *The development and treatment of childhood aggression* (pp. 411–438). Hillsdale, NJ: Erlbaum.

Olweus, D. (1992) . Bullying among schoolchildren: Intervention and prevention. In R. Peters, R. McMahon, & V. Quinsey (Eds.), *Aggression and violence throughout the lifespan* (pp. 100–125). London: Sage.

Olweus, D. (1993). *Bullying at school: What we know and what we can do.* London: Blackwell.

Olweus, D. (1994). Bullying at school: Long-term outcomes for the victims and an effective school base intervention program. In L. Huesmann (Ed.), *Aggressive behavior: Current perspectives* (pp. 97–130). New York: Plenum.

Olweus, D. (1996). Bully/victim problems at school: Facts and effective intervention: Reclaiming children and youth. *Journal of Emotional and Behavioral Problems, 5*(1), 15–22.

Olweus, D. (1997). Bully/victim problems at school: Facts and interventions. *European Journal of Psychology of Education, 12,* 495–510.

Olweus, D. (2001). Peer harassment: A critical analysis and some important issues. In J. Juvonen & S. Graham (Eds.), *Peer harassment in school: The plight of the vulnerable and victimized* (pp. 138–165). New York: Guilford.

O'Moore, A., Kirkham, C., & Smith, M. (1997). Bullying behavior in Irish schools: A nationwide study. *Irish Journal of Psychology, 18,* 141–169.

Patterson, G. (1982). *Coercive family processes.* Eugene, OR: Castalia.

Patterson, G. (1986). The contribution of siblings to training for fighting: A microsocial analysis. In D. Olweus, J. Block, & M. Radke-Yarrow (Eds.), *Development of antisocial and prosocial behavior: Research, theories, and issues* (pp. 235–261). New York: Academic Press.

Pelligrini, A. (1998). Bullies and victims in school: A review and call for research. *Journal of Developmental Psychology, 19,* 165–176.

Pelligrini, A., & Long, J. (2002). A longitudinal study of bullying, dominance, and victimization during the transition from primary school through secondary school. *British Journal of Developmental Psychology, 73,* 1119–1133.

Perry, D., Perry, L., & Kennedy, E. (1992). Conflict and the development of antisocial behavior. In C. Shantz and W. Hartup (Eds.), *Conflict in child and adolescent development* (pp. 301–329). New York: Cambridge University Press.

Prinstein, M., Boergers, J., & Vernberg, E. (2001). Overt and relational aggression in adolescents: Social-psychological adjustment of aggressors and victims. *Journal of Clinical Child Psychology, 30,* 479–491.

Rigby, K. (1998). The relationship between reported health and involvement in bully/victim problems among male and female secondary school students. *Journal of Health Psychology, 3*(4), 465–476.

Rigby, K. (2000). Effects of peer victimization in schools and perceived social support on adolescent well-being. *Journal of Adolescence, 23,* 57–68.

Rigby, K., & Slee, P. (1991). Bullying among Australian school children: Reported behavior and attitudes to victims. *Journal of Social Psychology, 131,* 615–627.

Rivers, I., & Smith, P. (1994). Types of bullying behaviors and their correlates. *Aggressive Behavior, 20,* 359–368.

Ross, C., & Ryan, A. (1990). *Can I stay in today miss? Improving the school playground.* Stoke-on-Trent, UK: Trentham Books.

Salmivalli, C., Lagerspetz, K., Bjorkqvist, K., Österman, K., & Kaukianinen, A. (1996). Bullying as a group process: Participant roles and their relations to social status within the group. *Aggressive Behavior, 22,* 1–15.

Schwartz, D., Dodge, K. A., & Coie, J. D. (1993). The emergence of chronic peer victimization in boy's play groups. *Child Development, 64,* 1755–1772.

Seeger, M., Barton, E., Heyart, B., & Bultnyck, S. (2001). Crisis planning and crisis communication in the public schools: Assessing post-Columbine responses. *Communication Research Reports, 18,* 375–83.

Selman, R. (1980). *The growth of interpersonal understanding: Developmental and clinical analyses.* San Diego, CA: Academic Press.

Simmons, R. (2002). *Odd girls out: The hidden culture of aggression in girls.* New York: Harcourt.

Slee, P. T. (1995). Peer victimization and its relationship to depression among Australian primary school children. *Personality and Individual Differences, 18,* 57–62.

Smith, P., & Sharp, S. (1994). *School bullying: Insights and perspectives.* London: Routledge.

Smith, P. K., & Shu, S. (2000). What good schools can do about bullying: Findings from a survey in English schools after a decade of research and action. *Childhood, 7,* 193–212.

Song, S., & Swearer, S. (2002, February). *An ecological analysis of bullying in middle school: Understanding school climate across the bully-victim continuum.* Paper presented at the Annual Convention of the National Association of School Psychologists, Chicago.

Stevens, V., deBourdeaudhuij, I., & Van Oost, P. (2000). Bullying in Flemish schools: An evaluation of anti-bullying intervention in primary and secondary schools. *British Journal of Educational Psychology, 70,* 195–210.

Sutton, J., Smith, P., Smith, J., & Swettenham, J. (1999). Social cognition and bullying: Social inadequacy or skilled manipulation? *British Journal of Developmental Psychology, 17*(3), 435–450.

Taylor-Greene, S., Brown, D., Nelson, L., Longton, J., Gassman, T., Cohen, J., et al. (1997). School-wide behavioral support: Starting the year off right. *Journal of Behavioral Education, 7,* 99–112.

Thomas, A., & Chess, S. (1977). *Temperament and development.* New York: Brunner/Mazel.

Todd, A., Horner, R., & Sugai, G. (1999). Self-monitoring and self-recruited praise: Effects on problem behavior, academic engagement, and work completion in a typical classroom. *Journal of Positive Behavior Interventions, 1,* 66–76.

Vossekuil, B., Fein, R., Reddy, M., Borum, R., & Modzeleski, W. (2002). *The final report and findings of the safe school initiatives: Implications for the prevention of school attacks in the United States.* Washington, DC: U.S. Secret Service and U.S. Department of Education.

Wachtel, P. (1973). Psychodynamics, behavior therapy and the implacable experimenter: An inquiry into the consistency of personality. *Journal of Abnormal Psychology, 83,* 324–34.

Walker, H., Kavanagh, K., Stiller, B., Golly, A., Severson, H., & Feil, E. (1998). First steps to success: An early intervention approach for preventing school antisocial behavior. *Journal of Emotional and Behavioral Disorders, 6,* 66–80.

Whitney, I., & Smith, P. K. (1993). A survey of the nature and extent of bully/victim problems in junior/middle and secondary schools. *Educational Research, 35,* 3–25.

Yoon, J., Barton, E., & Taiariol, J. (2004). Relational aggression in middle school: Educational implications of developmental research. *Journal of Early Adolescence, 24*(3), 303–318.

Yoon, J., & Kerber, K. (2003). Bullying: Elementary teachers' attitudes and intervention strategies. *Research in Education, 69,* 27–35.

Zehr, M. A. (2001, May 16). Legislatures take on bullies with new laws. *Education Week* [Electronic version]. Retrieved from http://www.edweek.org

Index